# Outlandish Scotland Journey

# Part One

A Novel Holiday Travel Guidebook

By CD Miller

# Outlandish Scotland Journey
# Part One
## A Novel Holiday Travel Guidebook

By CD Miller

**Published by:**
A Novel Holiday Travel Guidebooks
Ashland, NE  68003
USA
http://www.anovelholiday.com

**Print on Demand Paperback Book Distributor:**
Lightning Source
https://www.lightningsource.com/

**eBook Distributor:**
Amazon Kindle Direct Publishing
https://kdp.amazon.com/

All rights reserved. No part of this book may be reproduced or transmitted in any form or by any means, electronic or mechanical—including photocopying, recording, or any information storage and retrieval system—without written permission from the author, except for the inclusion of brief quotations in a review.

The publisher and author(s) of *Outlandish Scotland Journey* have taken great care to ensure that all information provided is correct and accurate at the time of manuscript submission. Unfortunately, errors and omissions—whether typographical, clerical or otherwise—sometimes occur. If you find an error or omission, please Email us and report it.
novelholiday@gmail.com

Changes in real-world site information will inevitably occur. As aptly stated by renowned travel guidebook author **Rick Steves**: "Guidebooks begin to yellow even before they're printed." For instance, the ticket and entry fees cited are those that were in effect during our last pass at researching each Outlandish site.

Users of any A Novel Holiday travel guidebook are advised to access the Internet links provided within each chapter in order to obtain the most up-to-date information during the planning of your Outlandish Scotland Journey.

**All fees cited in this book are provided in British Pounds (£).**
Use a free Internet currency converter—such as the one offered by Oanda—to obtain US Dollar or other foreign exchange rates, remembering that currency exchange rates change daily.
https://www.oanda.com/currency/converter/

The publisher and author(s) of *Outlandish Scotland Journey* hereby disclaim any liability to any party for loss, injury, or damage incurred as a direct or indirect consequence of errors, omissions, or post-manuscript-submission information changes, whether such errors, omissions, or changes result from negligence, accident, or any other cause.

Copyright © 2019 by Charly D Miller,
A Novel Holiday Travel Guidebooks Publishing Company
Printed in the United States of America
   ISBN 978-1-938285-07-3

Publisher's Cataloging-in-Publication Data
Miller, Charly D, 1956 -
Outlandish Scotland Journey
by Charly D Miller.
   p. cm.
         ISBN 978-1-938285-07-3 (softbound, all 7 Parts)
            (All softbound books include Index.)
         ISBN 978-1-938285-32-5 (softbound Part 1)
         ISBN 978-1-938285-06-6 (eBook Part 1) $3.99
         ISBN 978-1-938285-33-2 (softbound Parts 2 & 3)
         ISBN 978-1-938285-08-0 (eBook Part 2) $3.99
         ISBN 978-1-938285-09-7 (eBook Part 3) $2.99
         ISBN 978-1-938285-35-6 (softbound Part 4)
         ISBN 978-1-938285-11-0 (eBook Part 4) $5.99
         ISBN 978-1-938285-36-3 (softbound Parts 5 & 6)
         ISBN 978-1-938285-26-4 (eBook Part 5) $5.99
         ISBN 978-1-938285-27-1 (eBook Part 6) $0.00
            (Offered for Free on our website)
         ISBN 978-1-938285-38-7 (softbound Part 7)
         ISBN 978-1-938285-29-5 (eBook Part 7) $3.99
   1. Travel Guides—United Kingdom—.
   I. Title.
   DA870 .M460 2019

# Table of Contents

## Introduction

About *Outlandish Scotland Journey* (OSJ) — vi
OSJ Parts and Outlandish Site Numbers
OSJ Site Rating Icons
The Outlanderite Oath
Outlandish Extras
OSJ Fee Examples

## PART ONE: Sites between Edinburgh & Inverness

| | |
|---|---|
| Introduction | 1 |
| Culross Village, Site #1 | 2 |
| Charlestown Lime Kilns, Site #2 | 32 |
| Aberdour Castle, Site #3 | 37 |
| Dysart Harbor, Site #4 | 47 |
| Balgonie Castle, Site #5 | 54 |
| Falkland Village, Site #6 | 59 |
| Tibbermore Parish Church, Site #7 | 84 |
| Highland Folk Museum, Site #8 | 91 |
| Ruthven Barracks, Site #9 | 101 |

## Appendices

| | |
|---|---|
| Outlandish Scotland Extras | 105 |
| Disclaimers | 107 |
| Acknowledgements | 109 |
| Photography Credits | 110 |
| Index | 113 |
| The End | 115 |

# Introduction

## About Our Travel Guidebook

*Outlandish Scotland Journey* (OSJ) is designed to guide **Outlanderites** to a variety of real-world places:
- Scottish locations mentioned in Diana Gabaldon's first three novels (*Outlander*, *Dragonfly in Amber*, and *Voyager*).
- Scottish sites that inspired—or resemble—Diana's grandly-evocative, fictional location descriptions.
- Scottish film sites seen on screen in the STARZ network *Outlander* TV series.
- Scottish places where significant events occurred during the 1745 Jacobite rebellion—sometimes earlier Jacobite-related events.

## OSJ Parts and Outlandish Site Numbers

We present 65 Outlandish Scotland sites in our travel guidebook, grouped together based on the area in which they are found. Because we determined seven different Outlandish areas of Scotland (one of which includes a film site in Northwestern England), our guidebook is divided into Seven Parts.

Outlandish Scotland parts and sites are numbered in order of their location, as encountered if you begin your journey at Edinburgh Airport and head north toward Inverness. Part 1 covers eight film sites and one Outlandish location between the two cities. After Inverness (Part 2), visit the Scottish West Highlands (Part 3), followed by the Stirling area (Part 4), and *then* head to Edinburgh (Part 5). Three extra sites in Aberdeenshire (Part 6) are followed by Part 7, which includes the City of Glasgow, Southwestern Scotland, and Northwestern, England.

## Why not visit the city of Edinburgh first?

Visiting Edinburgh requires more walking than any other OSJ site. The most Outlandish parts of the city line steep streets, and you may occasionally have to slog up long and arduous flights of steps. If you spend the first few days of your holiday in a place that demands an inordinate amount of walking, you'll end up *limping* your way through subsequent sites—literally.

Even normally active, physically fit Outlanderites may suffer from blisters if they tackle Edinburgh on the first days of an Outlandish Scotland Journey. Few people are accustomed to such vigorous walking, all day long.

Saving Edinburgh for the midpoint or end of an Outlandish Scotland Journey will allow your feet to gradually become used to the activity.

# Introduction

## Outlandish Scotland Journey Site Rating Icons

Not all Outlandish Scotland sites are places even the most diehard Outlanderite will want to visit—especially those strapped for time. During our research, we assessed each site critically and assigned it a rating based on a number of factors, including:
- How important is it to the novels?
- How conveniently can it be visited?
- If a film site, is it easy to recognize what was seen on screen?
- Does the site offer particularly marvelous non-*Outlander* aspects or activities?

Our **Great Site** icon indicates an Outlandish site you don't want to miss.

Our **Might Be Fun** icon identifies places that may not be worth visiting. Each Might-Be-Fun Site chapter has an explanation of why it received that rating.

Our **Skip It** icon is assigned to places we feel should be skipped. The chapter explains why. We provide addresses or SatNav/GPS coordinates for Skip-It sites, but don't offer directions for finding them. Happily, Outlanderites divinely inspired to visit a Skip-It site can investigate the location using links we provide within the chapter.

# Outlandish Scotland Journey

## The Outlanderite Oath

It is important that all Outlanderites be as polite as possible when visiting Outlandish Scotland sites. It only takes *one* noisy or disrespectful fan to ruin the reception received by all those who visit thereafter. Please be the very best Outlander Ambassador you can be, and abide by the Outlanderite Oath everywhere you go.

> **THE OUTLANDERITE OATH:**
> **I solemnly swear, by all that I hold dear, that I will *NOT***
> - Trespass on private property.
> - Disturb the peace by engaging in obstreperous speech or indelicate actions—such as littering or destruction of local flora and fauna.
> - Photograph the faces of any residents or visitors present without their express permission.
> - Or, in any other way, represent *Outlander* fans as folk unworthy of being invited back.
>
> If ever I should violate this vow, may the Scottish sky open up and my heart be pierced with a bolt of white-hot lightning.

## OutlanderLinks

OutlanderLinks are PDFs that contain the website links cited within OSJ front and back matter sections, and within every Outlandish Site chapter. These files are posted free of charge on our website.

OutlanderLinks PDFs are designed to enable those who purchase the paperback—or those who buy an OSJ eBook, but use an eReader that cannot conveniently access the Internet—to easily explore the website links provided within the *Outlandish Scotland Journey* travel guidebook.

After opening an OutlanderLinks PDF on your computer or tablet, you can simply *click on* each link, rather than having to type website addresses into your Internet browser.

Many OutlanderLinks PDFs also include site coordinates or addresses, as well as public transportation information. By providing this information in a PDF, you can copy-and-paste these items as needed.

Furthermore, the special Maps we created for several Outlandish sites are posted in the OutlanderLinks directory.

## Outlandish Scotland Journey Maps

Some sites require special maps to best be able to find their *Outlander*-associated locations. For other sites, maps are helpful to developing a sense of direction and deciding upon visiting order. We create Outlandish maps with Google Maps screenshot segments, enhance them by adding *Outlander*-associated site indicators, and post them in the **OutlanderLinks** directory.

# Introduction

## Outlandish Scotland Extras

To provide Outlanderites with *all* the information important to planning an Outlandish Scotland Journey—yet keep the size of our paperback from being too large to carry conveniently while touring—we created several informative PDF files and posted them free of charge on the Outlandish Scotland Extras directory of our website.
http://outlandishscotland.com/outlandish-scotland-extras/

### Outlander Insider Info
Special Outlandish information that may be helpful, including identification of fictional places you cannot visit, information about some of the Outlander tours available, and a Site Overview Table to help you plan your own itinerary.

### Outlandish Scotland Travel Tips
Everything any Outlanderite needs to know about planning and preparing for a vacation in Scotland—or elsewhere in the UK.

A list of the Outlandish Extras PDFs is available in the Appendix.

## Fee Examples

To give you an idea of what items may cost when you visit, we provide the site-fees in effect during our last round of research. Refer to the reference link(s) provided in each individual site chapter to learn the most current fees when planning your holiday.

### All fees cited in this book are provided in British Pounds (£).
Use a free Internet currency converter—such as the one offered by Oanda (link below)—to obtain US Dollar or other foreign exchange rates, remembering that currency exchange rates change daily.
http://www.oanda.com/currency/converter/

# Part One Introduction

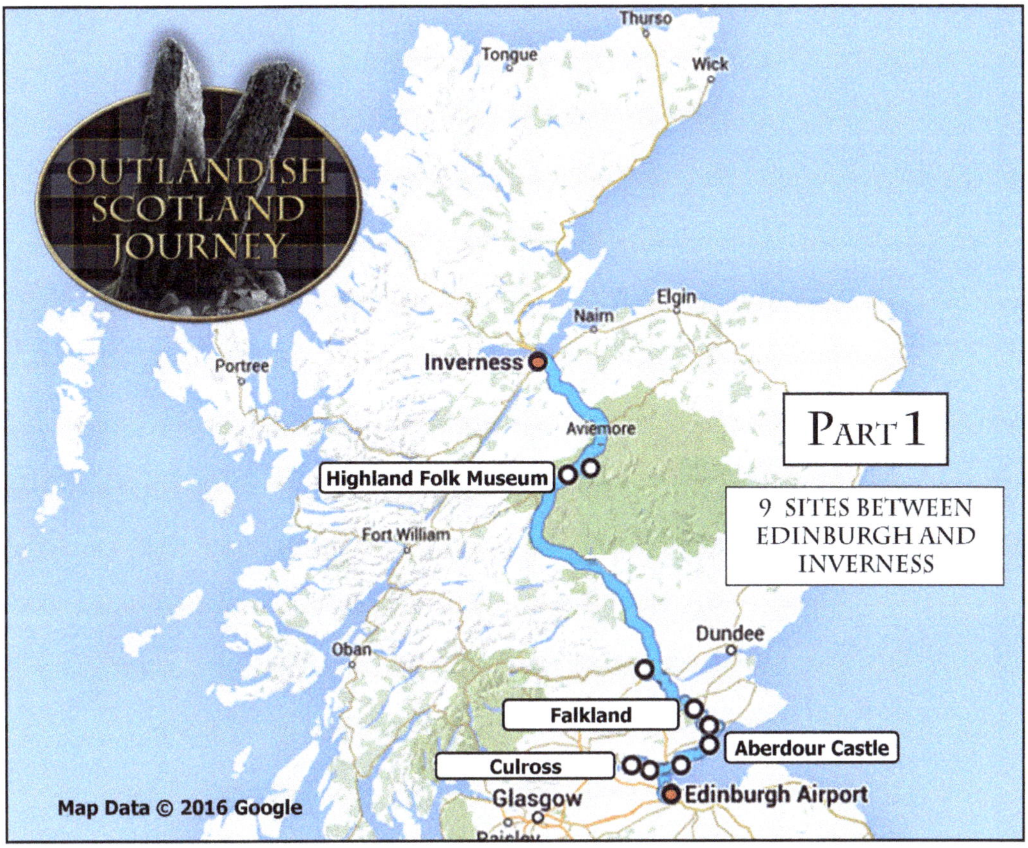

Part 1 of *Outlandish Scotland Journey* consists of
Nine Sites found between Edinburgh and Inverness.

 Four are rated **Great Site**.

 Four are rated **Might-Be-Fun**.

 One is rated **Skip-It**—but will become **Might-Be-Fun** when it reopens.

# Culross Village: Site #1

*Outlander* Season One *and* Two Film Site
Exterior Cranesmuir Scenes
and *MORE!*

[©2015 Joni Webb cotedetexas.blogspot.com segment (enhanced)]

    The lovely little village of Culross ("KOO-russ") is one of several small ports on the Firth of Forth—the estuary (firth) of Scotland's River Forth, north of Edinburgh, where it flows into the North Sea.
    What makes Culross special is that the village seems to have been frozen in time since the 1600s—long before Claire and Jamie could have trod o'er these cobblestones—largely because many buildings in the village have been owned and managed by the National Trust for Scotland (NTS) since 1932.
    "The Royal Burgh of Culross is … the most complete example in Scotland today of a Burgh of the 17th and 18th centuries. The Town House was built in 1626 and was the administrative centre of Culross with a tollbooth and witches' prison. The old buildings and cobbled streets create a fascinating time warp for visitors."
http://nts.org.uk/RoyalBurghofCulross

# Culross Village: Site #1

Because the Trust strives to keep the village untouched by the passage of time, and unmarred by visible evidence of modern technology, it comes as no surprise that Culross was selected as a major STARZ Outlander film site: the fictional village of Cranesmuir.

Amazingly enough, Ronald D. Moore (*Outlander* TV series creator and executive producer) managed to obtain permission to *repaint* the buildings surrounding the old town square for filming.

[©2015 Joni Webb cotedetexas.blogspot.com segment (enhanced)]

"The buildings at the Mercat Cross in the Royal Burgh of Culross, some of which are owned and managed by the National Trust for Scotland, are undergoing a temporary colour change. They have been specially painted for the filming of a major TV series currently in production in Scotland and will be returned to their usual state by early summer 2014. We actively encourage filming at our locations and are very pleased to be working with the production company, which has been consulting closely with the Trust's conservators and surveyors."

[*The Way Out* screenshot]   [©2015 Peter of marketplace.500px.com segment] Enhanced.

While some Outlanderites may be disappointed that the real-world buildings are a different color than those seen on screen, the structures weren't altered, and are easy to recognize.

# Outlandish Scotland Journey: Part One

## Outlander Season One Culross Village Film Site: Mercat Cross Square

On the west side of the old Culross market ("mercat") place stands the village's Mercat Cross. This type of monument was the symbol of a burgh's right to trade. Although the cross' shaft and head were reconstructed in 1902, its stepped, octagonal base is original—built in 1588. The unicorn carving on top was copied from Stirling's Mercat Cross.

> "As you wander through Culross, you'll see the Mercat Cross once the centre of life in town where trading was conducted and proclamations were read out."
> http://itraveluk.co.uk/content/602.html

In November of 2013, many memorable exterior Cranesmuir scenes for Season One of *Outlander* were shot in and around this square. Thus, the Culross Mercat Cross is frequently seen on screen.

- Episode 3, *The Way Out*
- Episode 10, *By the Pricking of My Thumbs*
- Episode 11, *The Devil's Mark*

Pillory and ear-nailing scenes in *The Way Out*.

The witch-burning pyre for *The Devil's Mark*.

# Culross Village: Site #1

The place Outlanderites are most eager to see, however, is the home of Geillis Duncan. As an 18th-century Procurator Fiscal, Arthur Duncan was the person solely responsible for investigating all crimes committed in the village's vicinity, as well as proclaiming the punishment for those he deemed guilty. Being such an important public official, Duncan's house would have been prominently situated on Cranesmuir's market square.

[*By the Pricking of My Thumbs* screenshot (enhanced)]

Appropriately, Geillis and Arthur Duncan's on-screen house is the large dwelling directly north of the Culross Mercat Cross.

[©2015 Joni Webb cotedetexas.blogspot.com segments (enhanced)]

As it happens, this dwelling contains Bishop Leighton's Study, which is included in the Culross Town House and Study Tour (more about that later). Bishop Leighton's Study is at the top of the building's Outlook Tower and has a small turret on its western side. To reach it, visitors must climb a steep and winding stone staircase.

# Outlandish Scotland Journey: Part One

[*The Way Out* screenshot segments (enhanced), above and below.]

Although Claire and Geillis are seen peering out one of the diamond-mullioned windows on the top floor, the only *interior* filming was their point-of-view shot, below.

Outlanderites who go on the Culross Town House and Study Tour will be able to peer out this very same window.

[*The Way Out* screenshot (enhanced)]

# Culross Village: Site #1

The entrance to Mrs. Fitz's family home—where her nephew, Tammas, lived—is on the west side of Little Causeway, the lane leading southeast from Mercat Cross square. (That's Geillis' house in the background, above and below.) All interior Fitz's family home scenes were shot on a sound stage set.

[*The Devil's Mark* screenshot (enhanced)]

Little Causeway is also where Claire and Geillis were jeered by villagers while being taken between the thieves' hole and court room … or (as seen above) when Geillis was being taken from the court room to the pyre.

[©2015 Joni Webb cotedetexas.blogspot.com (enhanced)]

# Outlandish Scotland Journey: Part One

## Culross Palace: Another Culross Village Film Site

Situated within the village, Culross Palace is actually a mansion house that was constructed between 1597 and 1611 by Sir George Bruce, the Laird of Carnock. Bruce was a local merchant who established a flourishing trade with other Firth of Forth ports, as well as several European ports bordering the English Channel.

"Many of the materials used in the construction of the palace were obtained during the course of Bruce's foreign trade. Baltic pine, red pantiles, and Dutch floor tiles and glass were all used. ... The palace features fine interiors, with decorative mural and ceiling painting, 17th and 18th century furniture and a fine collection of Staffordshire and Scottish pottery. Although never a royal residence, James VI visited the palace in 1617."
https://en.wikipedia.org/wiki/Culross_Palace

Culross Palace admission tickets are only available in the old Town House visitor centre. A palace audio tour can also be rented.

After entering the palace and watching a 10-minute orientation film, you are free to wander through it at your own pace. Docents are posted in each of the rooms to provide information and answer questions.

## *Outlander* Season One Film Sites Within the Palace

[©2006 Gary of itraveluk.co.uk (enhanced)]

Interior scenes for Geillis Duncan's parlor were filmed in the Withdrawing Room of Culross Palace. The room's paneled walls are painted a mossy green and adorned with antique oil paintings and Staffordshire plates. Though not seen in the Geillis parlor scenes shot here, filmmakers recreated the withdrawing room candelabra chandelier for her attic herb room set.

# Culross Village: Site #1

[*The Way Out* screenshot segments (enhanced), above and below.]

The Withdrawing Room's furnishings and accessories were replaced for filming, but you'll easily recognize the distinctive paneled walls and fireplace seen on screen when visiting Culross Palace.

The scenes of Jamie arriving to escort Claire back to Castle Leoch were shot at the other end of the withdrawing room, opposite from the fireplace.

[©2006 Gary of itraveluk.co.uk (enhanced)]   [©2013 uktour.files.wordpress.com segment]

# Outlandish Scotland Journey: Part One

Another Culross Palace room of Outlanderite interest is the Painted Chamber. Its barreled ceiling is covered with "many curiously painted pictures, illustrative of morality and virtue, with appropriate and quaint maxims in verse."
http://archaeologydataservice.ac.uk/catalogue/adsdata/arch-352-1/dissemination/pdf/vol_002/2_339_344.pdf

The panel seen above right bears the caption:
"Men's pleasures fond, do promeis only joyes.
Bot he that yeldes, at lengthe him self destroyes."

[*The Way Out* screenshot segments (enhanced), above and below.]

Above and below is Geillis' attic herb room set. (Note the Withdrawing Room's candelabra hanging at its center, above.) Supported by large, wooden struts, the set's barreled ceiling is different from that of the painted chamber. The painted panels seen between the struts, however, were clearly inspired by those you'll see when visiting Culross Palace.

Fittingly (for her character), Geillis' painted panels are less "moral and virtuous."

# Culross Village: Site #1

## *Outlander* Season Two Film Sites Within the Palace

In November of 2015 the *Outlander* cast and crew returned to Culross to film scenes for Season Two, Episode 11, "Vengeance Is Mine."

"The Palace High Hall was used for the Jacobite meeting where Jamie swears his oath to Prince Charlie. The Palace's Kings Room was used as Jamie and Claire's bedroom while visiting a village. The Palace's Kitchen and Pantry was used as a tavern."
http://www.nts.org.uk/Property/Royal-Burgh-of-Culross/

### The Culross Palace High Hall

"This is the High Hall at Culross Palace the first room you walk into when you visit and the main business and entertaining space in the Palace. It's design and decoration is ship like [another room with a barreled ceiling], a reminder of the importance of trade in [Sir George Bruce's] success."
https://www.facebook.com/RoyalBurghofCulross/photos/

[©2016 facebook.com/RoyalBurghofCuross ]   [*Vengeance Is Mine* screenshot segment (enhanced)]

In the screenshot above right, you can see that the cabinet and table that reside within the Culross Palace High Hall (photo above left) remained in place for filming.

[*Vengeance Is Mine* screenshot]   [©2015 BBC Radio] Segments, enhanced.

As for the fireplace at the opposite end of the Culross Palace High Hall, it is exactly as it appears on screen, as seen in the screenshot and photo above.

# Outlandish Scotland Journey: Part One

[Internet-posted pic ©Unknown]  [*Vengeance Is Mine* screenshot] Segments, enhanced.

**The Culross Palace Kings Room**
The Kings Room fireplace—seen above in both the room's photo and an *Outlander* screenshot—clearly identifies this room as the film site for Jamie and Claire's bedchamber.

[©2015 Tadeusz Czesław Sinica]  [*Vengeance Is Mine* screenshot (enhanced)]

**The Culross Palace Kitchen and Pantry**
A portion of the palace kitchen is seen in the photo above, left. Note the huge hearth. Above right is a screenshot showing Claire warming herself before a fire in that hearth, while dozing the Ram's Hedd Taverne common room on the night before she is taken by the Redcoats to Bellhurst Manor, "a big house owned by a rich Englishman."

[Internet-posted pic ©Unknown]  [*Vengeance Is Mine* screenshot] Segments, enhanced.

# Culross Village: Site #1

Above, left, is a photo we found that also was identified as the "Culross Palace kitchen." While that identification may or may not be accurate, the fabulous painted ceiling of this room is something you're sure to enjoy.

Furthermore, this room *is* a film site. The screenshot from Episode 211 (above, right) shows Jamie next to one of the windows seen in the photo of this room. This screenshot is from the scene where Dougal delivers a letter from O'Sullivan to Jamie, conveying the orders of Prince Charles Edward Stuart. The prince commands Jamie to lead his men to Inverness, where he is to "arrange winter quarters and obtain provisions."

> **Dougal:** "Exile is what it is. They want to be rid of us, rid of you. O'Sullivan fears that you have too much influence over the prince, and Murray, oh, he did naught to defend you. They want you and me gone and gone now."

Hopefully, the Culross Palace docent assigned to the room will regale you with tales of the *Outlander* Season Two filming that took place here.

**Why are some of the Culross Palace room photos we've published of such poor quality?**
Alas, photography isn't *allowed* inside Culross Palace (*or* inside the Town House and the Study). Many pieces found within are on loan to the National Trust, and they do not have the necessary agreements to allow photography.

Happily, visitors are free to snap pix anywhere *outside* the palace—such as in the garden and courtyard.

[©2013 Jessica Tivy segment (enhanced)]

## *Outlander* Season One Culross Village Film Site:
## Culross Palace Garden

In 1993, the NTS began restoring the Culross Palace Garden, creating a model 17th-century garden on the terraced slope behind the palace. Initially requiring more than a decade of dedicated work, the garden continues to be improved with each passing season.

> "A series of eight raised plots with interconnecting paths dressed in crushed mussel and cockle shells was created to support a wide range of [17th-century] period

# Outlandish Scotland Journey: Part One

vegetables including onions, peas, beans, skirret, kale, scorzonera and salsify. Most of the vegetables currently grown are the oldest varieties still commercially available, some of which are sourced through Garden Organic's Heritage Seed Library.

"A covered walkway supporting *Vitis vinifera* 'Ciotat' (a variety of the common grape vine) and mulberries separates the main productive garden from a small orchard of old Scottish fruit varieties and a collection of rare Scots Dumpy hens.

"… the garden has continued to evolve based on a developing understanding of 17th-century horticulture and garden design, with an even greater emphasis on period features. These include trellis fencing, bowers, covered seats, basket planters and historic tools."

http://buildingconservation.com/articles/garden-conservation/garden-conservation

[*The Way Out* screenshot (enhanced)]

Imagine Ron Moore's delight when he discovered that Castle Leoch's garden actually existed, and in a location already slotted for filming.

BTW: If "rare Scots Dumpy hens" caught your attention in the Culross Palace Garden description above, it is with good reason!

In chapter 126, page 715, of *Written in My Own Heart's Blood*—the eighth book in Diana's *Outlander* series—Claire travels to Savannah, Georgia, in November of 1778 and discovers Scots Dumpy hens at the farm where Jamie's printing press was stored.

> "What remarkable chickens those are," I said, stifling a small belch. The beer, of Mrs. Simpson's own production, was tasty but strong. The chickens in question were more than remarkable: they appeared to have no legs but to be trundling round the yard on their bottom sides, pecking at their corn with cheerful imperturbability.
>
> "Oh, aye," said Mrs. Simpson, nodding with pride. "My mother brought those—well, their great-great-grandmothers—with her from Scotland, thirty years a-gone. 'Creepies,' she always called them—but they've got a true name. Scots Dumpy, it is, or so a gentleman from Glasgow told me."
>
> "How very appropriate," I said, taking another sip of beer and peering at the chickens. They did after all *have* legs; just very short ones.

# Culross Village: Site #1

In chapter 139, Claire looks for Scots Dumpies when visiting the Beardsley's Trading Post. "I had some hopes of spotting a Scots Dumpy but found only the usual run of Dominiques and Nankins."

[©2013 Jessica Tivy (enhanced)]  [©2012 Lorna McInnes]

When visiting Culross Palace Garden, keep an eye out for the resident Scots Dumpies. Usually found industriously scratching and pecking near their henhouse in the orchard, they may be hiding *under* the henhouse if it's raining.

## *Outlander* Season Two Culross Village Film Site: The Culross Palace Courtyard

[©2012 Lorna McInnes]
Gate leading to the Culross Palace Courtyard

# Outlandish Scotland Journey: Part One

"The Palace Courtyard and main stairway was used as a village encampment where Claire pulls the tooth from a Scottish woman and Murtagh waits on Jamie finishing a meeting with Prince Charles. Look out for the colour of the Palace!"
http://www.nts.org.uk/Property/Royal-Burgh-of-Culross/

[*Vengeance Is Mine* screenshot (enhanced)]

To film portions of *Outlander* Episode 211, a large encampment was constructed within the Culross Palace courtyard. In the scenes shot looking *out* from the encampment (such as the screenshot above), the balls mounted atop the Culross Palace courtyard gateposts are easily recognized.

Also for these scenes, a few tents were erected in the triangular memorial plaza known as "Sandhaven" found immediately in front of Culross Palace. Additional encampment tents and the mountains that appear in the distance are CGI elements added in post production. When looking south from Culross Palace, the real-world view is completely different from that seen above.

[*Vengeance Is Mine* screenshot]   [©2002 Lyall Duffus] Segments, enhanced.

Claire's field hospital (and dentistry parlor) was constructed within the courtyard, just around the corner from the stone steps leading to Culross Palace's main entrance.

# Culross Village: Site #1

## *Outlander* Season Two Culross Village Film Site: The Lane Leading West from the Culross Palace Gate & the Bennet House

"The Bennet House was used as the outside of [a] tavern [in Episode 211]."
http://www.nts.org.uk/Property/Royal-Burgh-of-Culross/

**About The Bennet House**
The National Trust for Scotland purchased the Bennet House in early May of 2015. Within the next year they formulated plans to renovate it.

"Bennet House has been unoccupied for around 20 years and the damaging effects of Scottish weather, combined with a lack of regular maintenance and upkeep, have taken their toll on the building."
http://westfifevillages.co.uk/News17.htm

As of 2019, restoration has been completed!

**Finding the Bennet House:**
When leaving Culross Palace, turn right after passing through the palace gate and walk west along Little Sandhaven lane. The Bennet House lies only a few steps down that lane, directly across from (south of) Bessie's Café—a place we'll tell you more about, later.

[©2015 farm8.staticFlickr.com segment (enhanced)]  [©2016 Starz (enhanced)]

In the photo above left, you can see the signs posted in front of the old Bessie Bar's Tearoom on the left—the Bennet House is directly across from that.

Above right is a behind-the-scenes photo released by the Starz network. In that photo, you can see two individuals warming their hands atop the Bennet House steps, and can barely make out the "Ram's Hedd Taverne" sign that was mounted for filming. Hugh Munro is crouched at the bottom of the steps.

In this scene, one of the Redcoats who are escorting Claire (after having "rescued" her from a little church near Falkirk, where she had been held captive by evil Scottish persons) is just coming into view. The soldiers are taking her to an inn where they will spend the night before delivering her to a manor house owned by "a rich Englishman."

# Outlandish Scotland Journey: Part One

[Internet-posted pic ©Unknown] [*Vengeance Is Mine* screenshot] Segments, enhanced.

The inn's entrance was located on the west face of the Bennet House, where another Ram's Hedd Taverne sign was installed, along with a small wooden awning above the door. In the screenshot above, Hugh Munro—still crouched at the bottom of the Bennet House steps—is peering around the northwest corner, watching Claire being taken into the Inn.

[©2015 Internet-posted Fan Pic segments (enhanced)]

Lucky Outlanderites who visited Culross during the November of 2015 shoot were treated to sightings of the show's stars trotting about on horseback between scenes, and found them happy to pose for personal photos when not acting.

[*The Way Out* screenshot segment (enhanced)]

## *Outlander* Season One Culross Film Site: The West Kirk

The ruins of Culross' West Kirk are where Jamie and Claire were filmed exploring Cranesmuir's Black Kirk, in hopes of learning the cause of Tammas' affliction.

# Culross Village: Site #1

"Situated to the northwest of Culross in West Kirk Churchyard and surrounded by agricultural land, [West Kirk] was the former parish church of Culross. It was replaced by the Abbey Parish Church by an Act of Parliament of 1633. However, it appears that [West Kirk] had been out of use for some time before this, as the Act records that it was already in a ruinous condition.

"[West Kirk] is now roofless and a large tree grows inside the western end of the building and much ivy on the walls. The graveyard is surrounded by low rubble boundary walls, which are in a poor state of repair in several places, and is entered at the southeast corner, where there are square gatepiers. …

"There is a large variety of headstones and table stones within the graveyard dating from the seventeenth [to] nineteenth centuries. The earlier monuments display symbols of death and mortality and a number of trades are also depicted, such as farmer, mariner and miner."
scottishchurches.org.uk/sites/site/id/1641/name/Culross+West+Church+Culross+Fife

[*The Way Out* screenshot segments (enhanced), above and below.]

As very little set-dressing was required for filming, you'll easily recognize the places where Claire and Jamie strolled—especially the marvelous window seen below.

There are three different walking routes—and one driving route—for reaching West Kirk, as we'll explain in the Time & Travel section.

# Outlandish Scotland Journey: Part One

[Google Street View image segment (enhanced)]

## The Culross Town House

**A Must-Visit Place—Though Not a Film Site**
On your way to the Culross west car park, you'll drive by the triangular memorial plaza known as, "Sandhaven." At Sandhaven's northwestern point is Culross Palace (above, left). The building crowned with a clock tower at the plaza's eastern apex is the old Culross Town House.

The Town House dates back to 1626, when it was the village's legal and commercial center, as well as the local prison.
> "Upstairs, the fine Georgian interior of the council chambers often houses exhibitions, whilst next door is the old courtroom. Downstairs in the shop is the debtors' cell, where, unlike previous occupants, you may decide only to spend a few moments!"

http://www.culture24.org.uk/sc000044

Culross Palace admission and Town Tour tickets can only be purchased in the visitor centre on the ground floor of the Town House. Thus, this should be your first stop in the village. You'll also find the NTS gift shop here—which began offering a few *Outlander*-themed items in 2015.

**Operation Hours Culross Palace & Garden, Culross Town House**
- March 28th–May 31st: open Thurs to Mon, noon to 5pm
- June 1st–August 31st: open daily, noon to 5pm
- September 1st–30th: open Thurs to Mon, noon to 5pm
- October1st–31st: open Thurs to Mon, noon to 4pm
- **November 1st—March 27th: Closed**

**Operation Hours Culross Palace Garden (only)**
Same dates/hours as above, with additional opening times below
- Nov 5th–March 23rd: open daily, noon to 4pm
- Closed: Dec 24th–26th, and Jan 1st.

# Culross Village: Site #1

**Palace and Garden Admission**
- NTS Members, Discover Ticket & Scottish Heritage Pass holders: Free
- Adult: £10.50
- Concession (Seniors and Students): £7.50
- Family: £24.50
- One Parent Family: £18.00

**Town Tours**
- NTS members, Discover Ticket and Scottish Heritage Pass holders: £3
- All others: £4 with Palace ticket

**Garden-Only Admission**
- NTS members, Discover Ticket & Scottish Heritage Pass holders: Free.
- All others: £3.50.

https://www.nts.org.uk/visit/places/culross

See the **Free Entry Passes** PDF in the Outlandish Extras directory of our website for more info about NTS membership.
http://OutlandishScotland.com/FreeEntryPasses.pdf

## About the Town Tour

Upper floors of the Town House, and the interior of the building that contains Bishop Leighton's Study (Geillis' home on Mercat Cross square), can only be visited during one of the guided Town Tours. The tours are offered from April 1st through September 30th, on Mondays through Saturdays, at 2pm. Town Tours have room for up to 16 people and last approximately 45 minutes.

## Other Culross Places of Interest

Culross is a fabulously Outlandish site to visit because there are far more than merely *Outlander*-related places of interest in the village.

[©2014 FunkyEllasTravels.com]

# Outlandish Scotland Journey: Part One

**Culross Pottery and Gallery**
**The Biscuit Café and Village Shop**
Just a few steps west of the Town House is a working pottery with a local art gallery and shop. Open year-round, seven days a week, from 10am to 5pm, the Culross Pottery Gallery is housed in a building that once was a 17th-century granary.

"In the [downstairs] pottery, visitors can watch resident potter Camilla Garrett-Jones working with crafted and hand thrown pieces which are then fired in the kilns in the pottery. Pottery classes are also run here throughout the year."
http://culrosspottery.com/

In the upstairs gallery you can peruse, and purchase, the creations of local Culross artisans who work in a variety of mediums. Paintings, drawings, textiles, ceramics, metalwork, jewelry—and much more—are on offer.

Adjacent to the gallery is the Biscuit Café. Enjoy a cup of fresh-brewed coffee, or sip on one of their amazingly vast variety of teas. (The tea menu is several pages long!) If you're peckish, munch on scrumptious home-baked cakes or the host of hot and cold foods available—all fresh-made daily, from locally-sourced ingredients. During summer months you can enjoy your sip and sup while sitting outside in the café's gorgeous garden.

Also found here is the Village Shop. It sells a small selection of packaged groceries, whatever local fresh veggies are in season, as well as snacks and beverages (including wine) to go.

[©2015 farm8.staticFlickr.com]

**Bessie Bar's Hall**
Believed to have been the niece of Sir George Bruce (he who built Culross Palace), Bessie Bar was a widow woman and malter who also owned and operated a popular ale house

# Culross Village: Site #1

in Culross during the late 16th century. The property thought to have been her place of business is immediately west of the palace.

When the NTS took over management of this building in 2013, it was restored, painted the same ochre color as the palace, and operated as Bessie's Tearoom. Unfortunately, even though it garnered great reviews, Bessie's Tearoom was closed after the 2014 season.

Since then, it has reopened as **Bessie's Café**. The "Excellent" and "Very Good" reviews on TripAdvisor are mixed with a few complaints about the high prices of some items. Below is the owner's response to one such complaint.

"At Bessie's we have a plant based menu mainly vegetarian and suitable for vegan, with gluten free options. The one exception is the high welfare, free-range, organic Puddledub dry-cured bacon. This costs extra, and we are happy to pay the farmer extra to look after the animals in a humane manner. Our free range organic eggs are farmed in the same way at Scottstoon farm just outside Dundee. We at Bessie's think that the welfare of the animals we eat is worth the extra cost. ... We do not eat or sell animal products that are farmed in battery or factory conditions."
https://www.tripadvisor.com/Restaurant_Review-g1925511-d12240369-Reviews-Bessie_s_Cafe-Culross_Fife_Scotland.html

Visit the Bessie's Café Facebook page to discover current opening hours.
https://www.facebook.com/culrosspalace/

[©2012 Adam, walkingandcrawling.blogspot.com (enhanced)]

## The Red Lion Inn
Outlanderites who lodge near Culross will not want to miss the Red Lion Inn—the only public house currently operating in Culross.

"Phone for reservations to avoid disappointment."
http://redlionculross.co.uk/
https://www.facebook.com/pages/category/Pub/Red-Lion-Inn-Culross-171978689510709/

The Red Lion Inn occupies a building that dates from the late 16th century, when it was probably Culross' coaching inn.

# Outlandish Scotland Journey: Part One

"In Europe, from approximately the mid-17th century for a period of about 200 years, the **coaching inn**, sometimes called a **coaching house** or **staging inn**, was a vital part of the inland transport infrastructure, as an inn serving coach travelers."
https://en.wikipedia.org/wiki/Coaching_inn

A coaching inn offered overnight accommodation and meals for its lodgers. The biggest difference between a modern day motel and a coaching inn: few motels offer fuel and garage space for motor vehicles, whereas the feeding and housing of horses was a coaching inn requirement.

[©2012 Adam, walkingandcrawling.blogspot.com segments (enhanced)]

Open daily from noon to 9pm, you'll thoroughly enjoy the Red Lion Inn's old world ambience, the fine food and ales served here, as well as the ceiling paintings by Scottish artist, Douglas Cadoo.

"The painted ceiling in the bar area depicts scenes from 'Kidnapped' by Robert Louis Stevenson and in the dining area the ceiling shows local scenes and symbols associated with the Burgh of Culross."

The Red Lion Inn is located next to the Culross Post Office, barely two blocks east of Sandhaven plaza. Because parking at the Inn is limited, we strongly suggest leaving your car in the west car park and walking here.

[Google Street View image segment (enhanced)]

BTW: Signs mounted on the Culross Post Office (above left) proclaim it as being the local "Tobacconist, News Agent, and Confectioner." A pay phone can be found outside the building, should you need one.

# Culross Village: Site #1

[©2014 Michael Garlick]

### Culross Abbey Ruins and the Parish Church

The ruins of Culross Abbey stand on a hillside above the village, next to Culross Abbey Church, where weddings and Sunday services are still held.

Built on the site of a 6th-century Pictish church, Culross Abbey was founded in 1217 by Malcolm, 7th Earl of Fife, who brought Cistercian monks here from Kinloss Abbey.

"Much of the original [Abbey] remains, although a great deal of it is in ruins. [What once was] the monks' choir forms the present parish church, which has been in continuous use since 1633. Modernized in 1824, the parish church was restored in 1905 by Sir Robert Rowand Anderson."

https://scotlandschurchestrust.org.uk/church/culross-abbey

### Hours of Operation

- The grounds are open daily, from 10am to dusk in summer — 10am to 4pm in winter.
- Sunday Services are held at 11:30am.
- The Abbey Tearoom is open daily, May through September, from 11am to 4pm.

The Abbey's location is identified on our **Culross Area Map**. (Time & Travel section.)

The uphill walk from Mercat Cross square to the Abbey is approximately 352 yards (two tenths of a mile) long. Composed of steep and uneven cobblestones, this somewhat arduous walk can be slippery when wet.

Abbey parking is extremely limited, and restricted to those with "significant mobility difficulties" who make arrangements to park here.

http://culrossabbey.co.uk/

## Learn More About Culross:

- http://undiscoveredscotland.co.uk/culross/culross/
- https://en.wikipedia.org/wiki/Culross
- https://galleryofgardens.wordpress.com/2013/11/20/culross-palace-scotland/
- http://britainexpress.com/attractions.htm?attraction=965

To see additional photos of "Cranesmuir" and the "Black Kirk," go to the **Culross Village** and **Culross West Kirk** boards on our **Outlandish Scotland Journey Pinterest Site**:

https://pinterest.com/chasOSJ/culross-village/
https://pinterest.com/chasOSJ/culross-west-kirk/

# Outlandish Scotland Journey: Part One

## OutlanderLinks

All website addresses and coordinates found in this chapter (including those in the Time & Travel section, below) are available in the **Site #1 OutlanderLinks** PDF, posted free of charge on the **Part 1 OutlanderLinks** directory of our website.
http://OutlandishScotland.com/01OutlanderLinks.pdf

   Updated information available after *Outlandish Scotland Journey* is published will also be posted in this directory.

## Time & Travel: Culross

Please know that visiting Culross may be problematic for Outlanderites with mobility issues. There are uneven, cobbled streets throughout the village. Culross Palace, the Town House, and Bishop Leighton's Study contain uneven surfaces as well as spiral staircases. Culross Palace Garden is wheelchair accessible, but may be a challenge.

## Visiting Time

To fully enjoy all that Culross has to offer, schedule **6 hours** here.

   Yes, that's a long time. But, this fabulous little village is filled with marvelously Outlandish sites that you'll not want to miss.

If 6 hours is too long for your itinerary, chose carefully between the activities listed below. Each is prefaced by the *minimum* amount of time required to enjoy them.

- **1 hour:** A quick, unguided walk about the village—snapping pix at the Mercat Cross square film site—can be accomplished in a single hour.
- You can skip this hour if you go on the Town Tour—*unless* you want to peruse the NTS gift shop … or have a meal in the village … or visit any of the other Culross places of interest mentioned above. If that is the case, schedule at least an hour to do one or two of these things before or after the tour.
- **1 hour:** Take the Town Tour to be guided through the village and gain access to the building that played the part of Geillis Duncan's home. One hour includes time to snap Mercat Cross square pix, but doesn't allow time to visit the NTS gift shop—*unless* you skip the last part of the tour: the Town House upper floors.
- **1 hour:** Wander through Culross Palace, visiting the withdrawing room film site and the painted chamber that inspired Geillis' attic ceiling.
- **1 hour:** Meander through Culross Palace's 17th-century garden to experience Castle Leoch's garden and commune with the resident Scots Dumpies.
- If you're not interested in gardens (or chickens), this time allotment could be cut to **30 minutes.**
- **90 minutes:** Walk the country path to Culross' West Kirk—aka Cranesmuir's Black Kirk—and spend 30 minutes enjoying this site.
- **45 minutes:** Drive to West Kirk and spend 30 minutes at the Black Kirk film site.

**The Universal First Step for a Culross Visit:**
Upon arrival in Culross, head to the Town House visitor centre to learn the day's Town Tour time and purchase your palace and/or tour tickets. Schedule all other village visitations around the Town Tour time.

# Culross Village: Site #1

**Culross Location Coordinates**
- There are Two Car Parks in Culross
  Both car parks are free, with ample spaces available.
  **Culross West Car Park:** 56.054963, -3.633605
  The west car park is for cars only.
  **Culross East Car Park:** 56.055622, -3.623119
  The east car park is reserved for coach (bus) and motor home parking.
- **The Town House:** 56.055259, -3.630208
- **Culross Palace and Garden:** 56.055474, -3.630918
- **Mercat Cross Square:** 56.055639, -3.628349
- **West Kirk:** 56.059870, -3.639647
- **Culross Abbey and Abbey Church:** 56.058262, -3.626240

## Public Transportation Directions

Info for reaching Culross via bus and train is provided on the NTS webpage below:
https://www.nts.org.uk/visit/places/culross/getting-here

Alternatively use Traveline Scotland to plan your journey.
www.travelinescotland.com
www.travelinescotland.com/apps

## Driving Directions

Unfortunately, programming Culross west car park coordinates into your vehicle's SatNav/GPS device may not result in the best route for reaching the village. This is because the device probably won't recognize how extremely narrow the lanes that pass through Mercat Cross square are—Google Maps certainly doesn't. These lanes should be avoided.

Thus, we created a **Driving to Culross Directions** PDF, and posted it free of charge on the **Outlandish Extras** directory of our website.
http://OutlandishScotland.com/01CulrossDrivingDirections.pdf

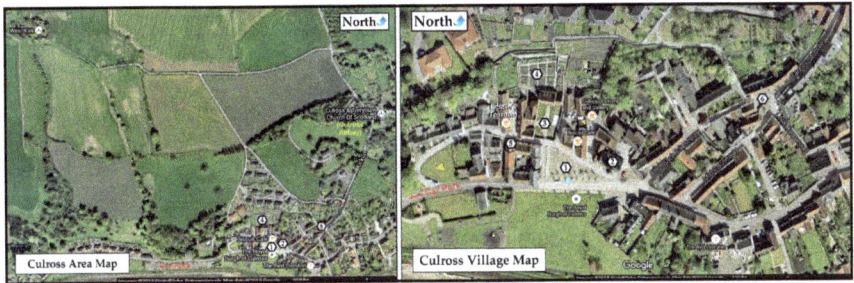

[Google Map segments (enhanced): ©2015 DigitalGlobe/Getmapping plc, ©2015 Google]

## Outlandish Scotland Journey Culross Maps

To assist all Outlanderites visiting Culross, we created five maps and posted them in one **Culross Maps** PDF.
http://OutlandishScotland.com/01CulrossMaps.pdf

# Outlandish Scotland Journey: Part One

Our **Culross Area Map** identifies the location of West Kirk, Culross Abbey, and the West Car Park in relationship to the village.

Our **Culross Village Map** identifies Outlandish sites within the village, as well as other Culross village places of interest.

**OSJ Culross Maps Key**
1. Sandhaven Memorial Plaza
2. The Town House Visitor Centre
3. Culross Palace & Courtyard
4. Culross Palace Garden
5. The Bennet House on Little Sandhaven lane
6. Mercat Cross Square

After parking in the west car park, go to the road and turn right to walk east to Sandhaven plaza and the Town House visitor centre. From there, use our Culross Village Map to find your way around.

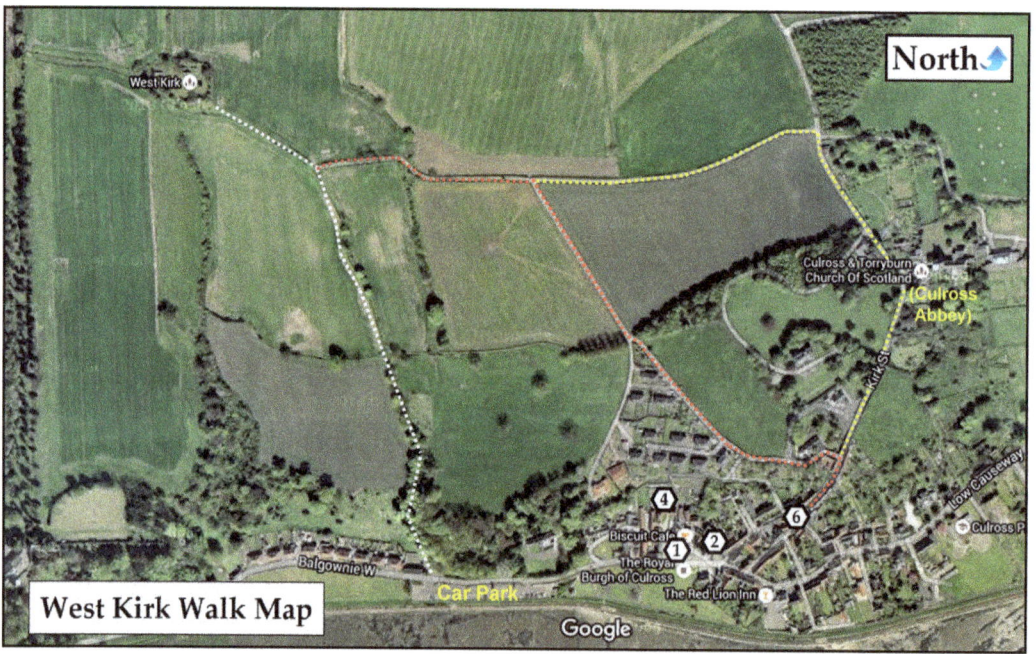

[Google Map segment (enhanced): ©2015 DigitalGlobe/Getmapping plc, ©2015 Google]

**The West Kirk Walk Map**
The best way to experience the Outlandish nature of the Black Kirk film site is to walk along the country path that leads there from the west car park.

However! Unless you arrive at the west car park at least 90 minutes before Culross Palace and the Town House open (long before the first Town Tour is scheduled), you should first walk into the village and visit the Town House visitor centre. Thus, our West Kirk Walk Map identifies two additional walking routes between Mercat Cross square the West Kirk film site.

# Culross Village: Site #1

**West Kirk Walk Map Key**
   **White Dot Route:**
   This is the country path that leads to West Kirk from the west car park. The path begins directly across the road from the car park's western entrance. This route is about a 30 minute one-way walk.

   **Red Dot Route:**
   This is the fastest route to West Kirk from Mercat Cross square—about a 35 minute one-way walk.

   **Yellow Dot Route:**
   Outlanderites who also wish to visit Culross Abbey should follow the White or Red Dot routes to West Kirk, then walk to the Abbey from there—along the Yellow Dot route. That way you'll not have to walk *up* the extremely steep, cobblestone lane between Mercat Cross square and the Abbey.

   The route leading back from the kirk to Mercat Cross square via the Abbey is about a 45 minute one-way walk—not counting time spent visiting the Abbey.

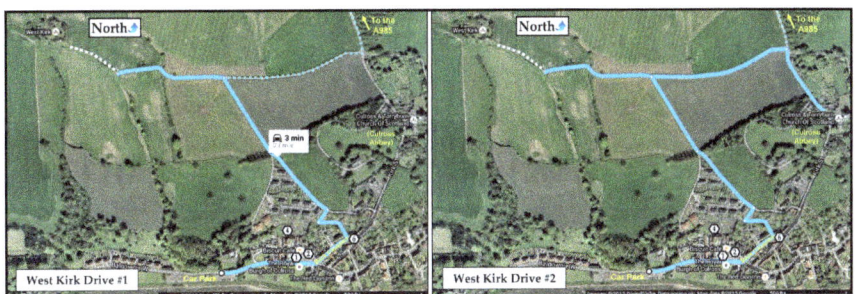

[Google Map segments (enhanced): ©2015 DigitalGlobe/Getmapping plc, ©2015 Google]

**Drive to West Kirk**
Our last two Culross maps are driving routes to West Kirk—and the Abbey—from the west car park.

Drive #1 shows the route to West Kirk, then back to the A985 when finished there (skipping the Abbey).

Mobility challenged Outlanderites who have called ahead to secure parking at the Abbey should use West Kirk Drive #2 to visit the Abbey after the kirk.

**Please Note:**
- Back Causeway does not connect with Mercat Cross square in a manner that allows you to drive across the square to Tanhouse Brae (which becomes Kirk Street), and then to the Abbey. Only those who walk up Back Causeway can enter Mercat Cross square from that lane.
- Avoid the extremely narrow lanes that travel through Mercat Cross square, as well as Kirk Street (the steep, cobblestone lane leading to the Abbey). Even if you'll not be visiting the West Kirk (gasp) before driving to the Abbey, we strongly suggest using Drive #2's route rather than driving through Mercat Cross square.

29

# Outlandish Scotland Journey: Part One

[©2015 Google Street View image segment (enhanced)]

**West Kirk Parking**
The last section of the unsigned roads leading to West Kirk—beginning where you turn left at the top of both driving routes (above)—is unpaved. Proceed with caution!

Rumor has it that an Outlanderite driving down the West Kirk dirt road suffered a dislodged fuel tank.
http://greatscotblog.com/tag/culross/

A much more likely hazard: the West Kirk dirt road may be an impassable mire of mud if recently soaked by heavy rain.

If the dirt road seems sloggy after pulling onto it—or you hear *anything* scuffing along your vehicle's undercarriage—stop and back straight out onto the paved road that runs east-west (above, right). Continue in reverse until you're well past the turn. Then, pull forward to park on the stone-wall-side of the road. (The hedge-side is bordered with flora.)

To ensure that you're not blocking the road, you should park so close to the stone wall that your front seat passenger has to climb out of the driver's door.

It's about a 3 minute walk to the West Kirk from this turn.

If the dirt road seems passable, continue carefully until you reach its end.

The road doesn't go all the way to the kirk and there is no official parking layby at its end. Be sure to park in manner that doesn't block a farmer's field access.

It's only a 1 minute walk from here to the West Kirk.

# Culross Village: Site #1

## Leaving Culross

To leave Culross from the West Kirk, simply drive east from where you parked until the road ends. Turn left and head north on Gallows Loan—an unsigned road. (This is where you turn right if driving to the Abbey.)

For Kincardine and points west, keep straight on Gallows Loan, heading northwest, until you reach the A985. Turn left there.

For points east—such as the other Part One Outlandish Scotland Journey sites—make a sharp right turn at the first intersection you encounter after turning northwest down Gallows Loan, and follow that road east. It soon will curve north and take you to the A985. Once there, turn right.

If you're heading to points east but somehow miss the sharp right turn and continue northwest on Gallows Loan, you'll still reach the A985. Turn right there.

If leaving Culross from the west car park, turn left and drive west from the car park to reach Kincardine and points west.

For points east, turn right and drive east from the car park on Low Causeway for 1.2 miles (approximately 4 minutes). Low Causeway ends at the B9037. There, make a very sharp left turn to take the B9037 west and north to the A985.

## Lodging in Culross

At this writing (2019), there doesn't seem to be any lodging option available *in* Culross. (The Red Lion Inn no longer offers rooms.)

Happily, there is a collection of Fife county guesthouse proprietors whose website is a great resource for finding a place to stay from which you can conveniently reach all of the first six Outlandish Scotland Journey sites.

> "All members of the 'A Stay in Fife' collection have been chosen for their high standards of hospitality, cleanliness and friendliness. Family owned and located throughout the county of Fife, they're some of the best bed & breakfasts on offer."
> http://astayinfife.co.uk/

If the info above doesn't work for you, see our **Scotland Lodging Tips** PDF.
http://OutlandishScotland.com/ScotlandLodgingTips.pdf

# Charlestown Lime Kilns: Site #2

*Outlander* Season One Film Site
Episode 14, "The Search"
Dougal's Cache of Jacobite Weapons and Supplies

[*Outlander* Season 1 screenshot segment (enhanced)]

In Season One, Episode 14—*The Search*—Gypsies give Claire a message that she thinks is from Jamie, identifying a remote cave meeting place. She and Murtagh rush to the meeting place, but find Dougal there instead.

FYI: The scenes fimed here were very darkly lit. We've lightened the screenshots as much as possible—so that you can recognize the lime kiln area—hence the poor quality.

Scenes of Claire and Murtagh dashing up a natural stone ramp to reach the meeting place were shot at a real-world cave formation found on the estate of **Barskimming**, a film site featured in our **Not Going to Go There** Outlandish Extra PDF.
www.OutlandishScotland.com/NotGoingThere.pdf

# Charlestown Lime Kilns: Site #2

[*Outlander* Season 1 screenshots (enhanced)]

Footage of Claire and Murtagh entering the cave also was filmed at the Barskimming cave formation. It is only after Dougal turns a corner to lead them deeper into the "cave" that the Charlestown Lime Kilns location is seen on screen.

[*Outlander* Season 1 screenshot segment (enhanced)]

This is Dougal's hiding place for the cache of weapons and supplies he's been collecting for the Jacobite cause. This also is where Dougal tells them that Jamie was captured by the English, and has already been sentenced to hang in Wentworth Prison.

## About the Film Site

Because these *Outlander* scenes were shot within a complex of "lime kilns," the village of Limekilns is often misrepresented as being the film site location. It is not. Filming occurred in the Charlestown lime kilns, only a mile or so west of Limekilns, Scotland.

The first nine Charlestown lime kilns were built in 1777 to replace those that existed in the village of Limekilns. In 1792, five more kilns were added, bring the total number of kilns at this site to fourteen. The Charlestown lime kilns ceased operation in 1956, and fell into decay. Restoration efforts began in 1990, but only a portion of the complex is considered safe to enter today.

# Outlandish Scotland Journey: Part One

[Internet-posted pix, ©Unknown (enhanced)]

The Charlestown Lime Kilns film site receives a **Might-Be-Fun** rating because:
- Access is only allowed to a small section of the complex. The vast majority is fenced off and posted with "Danger—Keep Out" signs.
- With the set dressing props long gone, the site looks very little like what was seen on screen. Most Outlanderites will be happier spending their holiday time visiting more recognizable film sites.
- Why not a **Skip It** rating? Stopping at the lime kilns film site while enroute from Culross (Site #1) to Aberdour Castle (Site #3) only adds 20 minutes to that drive. If you keep your Charlestown Lime Kilns visit to 30 minutes, the site adds only an hour to your itinerary.

## Learn More About Charlestown and its Lime Kilns:
- https://en.wikipedia.org/wiki/Charlestown,_Fife
- http://undiscoveredscotland.co.uk/charlestown/charlestown/
- https://fifephotosandart.wordpress.com/2015/09/21/charlestown-harbour-and-lime-kilns-fife/
- https://fifephotosandart.wordpress.com/2015/08/28/limekilns-fife/
- https://heritagelandscapecreativity.wordpress.com/tag/new-lanark/
- http://scotlime.org/

To see additional photos of this site, go to the **Charlestown Lime Kilns** board on our **Outlandish Scotland Journey Pinterest Site**:
https://www.pinterest.com/chasOSJ/charlestown-lime-kilns/

# Charlestown Lime Kilns: Site #2

## OutlanderLinks

All website addresses and coordinates found in this chapter (including those in the Time & Travel section, below) are available in the **Site #2 OutlanderLinks** PDF, posted free of charge on the **Part 1 OutlanderLinks** directory of our website.
http://OutlandishScotland.com/02OutlanderLinks.pdf

   Updated Charlestown Lime Kilns information available after *Outlandish Scotland Journey* is published will also be posted in this directory.

## Time & Travel: Charlestown

Charlestown lies north of Edinburgh, across the Firth of Forth bridge.
   Although it is as easy to stop at Charlestown while driving *to* **Culross (Site #1)**, we think it best to begin your holiday with a **Great Site**, rather than a Might-Be-Fun site. Those who wish to visit the Charlestown lime kilns can conveniently do so when driving from Culross to **Aberdour Castle (Site #3)**.

**Visit Time:** 30 minutes
That ought to be sufficient to visit the accessible lime kilns section and snap a few pix.

**Hours of Operation:** None
This is an unmanaged public place without fees, guidance, or facilities of any kind. Keep in mind, however, that the lime kilns' interior is not illuminated. Thus, it is best to visit during the brightest time of day.

**Admission Fees**
As an unmanaged public place, there is no charge for visiting the Charlestown Lime Kilns.

[©2013 M J Richardson]   [©2014 Heritage Landscape Creativity]

## Driving Directions

**Charlestown Limekilns Site Coordinates:** 56.035594, -3.503375
These coordinates are for the approximate center of the Charlestown lime kilns complex — the one place where access is allowed. Look for the small section that isn't fenced in. (Photo above, left.) There's also a Charlestown lime kilns information sign here.

# Outlandish Scotland Journey: Part One

[Google Street View image segment (enhanced)]

**Car Park Coordinates:** 56.035579, -3.503280
There is a very small parking area approximately 1/10th of a mile before reaching the Charlestown lime kilns access point. Because this road is a dead-end, the kilns are always approached from the east. Thus, you'll see the parking area before reaching the kilns.

[Google Street View image segment (enhanced)]

**Alternate Parking Coordinates:** 56.035615, -3.505076
If the small eastern parking area is full, continue a short distance beyond (west of) the Charlestown lime kilns access point. There you'll find room to park half-on the sidewalk—facing either direction. Because the grassy area seen above allows pedestrians plenty of room to walk around a parked car, it is highly unlikely that you'll be ticketed for obstruction, especially since you won't be there for long.

# Aberdour Castle: Site #3

*Outlander* Season One Film Site
The Abbey of Ste. Anne de Beaupré

[©2008 Andy Hawkins segment (enhanced)]

Aberdour Castle is located in the Fife county village of Easter Aberdour and managed by Historic Scotland. It may be the oldest standing masonry castle in Scotland.

"Hidden away in [Aberdour Castle's] extensive complex are the remains of a two-storey hall-house. Its cubed ashlar masonry walls are remarkably similar to those in the nearby parish church of St Fillan's, dated to the mid 12th century. … The splayed base course and clasping angle-buttresses at the corners are further evidence of Norman mason work.

"Hitherto the accolade of oldest standing castle in Scotland has gone to Castle Sween, in far-off Argyll, which is dated to the end of the 12th century. However, Aberdour's hall-house could conceivably have been built around 1150 …"
www.historicenvironment.scot/visit-a-place/places/aberdour-castle-and-gardens/

Filming for the *Outlander* Season 1 finale events that occurred in the novel's Abbey of Ste. Anne de Beaupré took place at Aberdour Castle in September of 2014.

"The Abbey of Ste. Anne de Beaupré is a fictional Benedictine monastery located on the northern coast of France. One of Jamie's six Fraser uncles, Alexander, is abbot there. Claire and Murtagh bring Jamie there to recover after his ordeal at Wentworth Prison."
http://outlander.wikia.com/wiki/Abbey_of_Ste._Anne_de_Beaupre

# Outlandish Scotland Journey: Part One

Interestingly enough, Aberdour Castle wasn't a stand-in for the fictional French location. With Diana's blessing, the abbey was moved to Scotland for the television series, and its name was never mentioned onscreen.

For more info about the decision to relocate the Abbey for TV, see our You Can't Get There From Here PDF, posted free of charge on the **Outlandish Extras** directory of our website. http://OutlandishScotland.com/YouCantGetThere.pdf

[*Outlander* Season 1, Episode 16 screenshot (enhanced)]

Scenes in Jamie's sick room were shot on a sound stage set, but its design was heavily influenced by Aberdour Castle's 16th-century architecture. All other abbey action was filmed on location in September of 2014.

[*Outlander* Season 1, Episode 16 screenshot (enhanced)]

Exterior abbey scenes were shot in the area along Aberdour Castle's southern face.

## Aberdour Castle: Site #3

[©2008 Andy Hawkins segment (enhanced)]

This film site is easy to recognize, thanks to the corner-mounted sundial on the easternmost building (seen above as well as in the previous screenshot) and the stone wall that overlooks the Aberdour Castle's terraced gardens.

[*Outlander* Season 1, Episode 16 screenshot segment (enhanced)]

When visiting, you can recreate the screenshot of Claire and company looking out over the gardens. Since your photographer will be standing in the garden on the opposite side of the wall, and snapping from a lower viewpoint than the crane-shot above, the picnic tables found in the film site area won't be seen behind you.

Interior abbey scenes were filmed in the castle's Stables, Long Gallery, and Old Kitchen. When you purchase your admission ticket and guidebook, ask a staff member to point out these places on the castle diagram.

# Outlandish Scotland Journey: Part One

[*Outlander* Season 1, Episode 16 screenshot (enhanced)]

You'll recognize the film site for the screenshot above the minute you step beyond this room's medieval, iron-studded door.

[©2010 Unda J]

This is the western-most room of the castle's East Range and can be entered from the exterior film site.

The Aberdour Castle Stables were used to film the abbey "passageway" where Claire fainted and fell into Murtagh's arms. The stable's medieval, iron-studded door doesn't open flush to the ground, as does the one in the East Range room. Watch your step!

# Aberdour Castle: Site #3

[©2013 Gavin of bikelove-scotland blogspot segment (enhanced)]

Set-dressing elements hid the stall and disguised the stable's width.

[*Outlander* Season 1, Episode 16 screenshot segments (enhanced) above and below]

# Outlandish Scotland Journey: Part One

[©2015 Joni Webb cotedetexas.blogspot.com segment (enhanced)]

The chapel set where Claire revealed everything to Father Anselm was built at one end of the Long Gallery of Aberdour Castle's East Range.

[*Outlander* Season 1, Episode 16 screenshot (enhanced)]

## Other Aberdour Castle Aspects of Interest

[©2008 Andy Hawkins]

# Aberdour Castle: Site #3

**The Terraced Garden**

Aberdour Castle's terraced garden was discovered during archaeological investigations undertaken by Historic Scotland between 1977 and 1980. It dates from at least 1540, and is comprised of four broad L-shaped terraces.

The high retaining walls were rebuilt in 1981. Unfortunately, because no evidence of the 16th-century planting schemes was found, the terraces were simply laid with grass.

[©2013 Gavin of bikelove-scotland blogspot (enhanced)]  [©2008 Andy Hawkins]

The terraces overlook an orchard dating from the late 1600s, which *has* been restored and grows more lovely every year.

The crowning glory of the terraced garden, however, is the 16th-century beehive-shaped doocot (dovecote) or pigeon house. Its purpose was to provide the household with a steady supply of fresh eggs and meat.

Containing approximately 600 nesting boxes, the Aberdour Castle doocot is 30 feet (9 meters) high. It rises in four steps, which are divided by "rat courses"—projecting ribs intended to prevent rodents from gaining entry.

[©2013 Gavin of bikelove-scotland blogspot (enhanced)]

Inside, you can see the nesting boxes up close, with this spectacularly geometric view when looking up through the small, circular opening at the doocot's apex.

# Outlandish Scotland Journey: Part One

[*Outlander* Season 1, Episode 16 screenshot segments (enhanced)]

**St. Fillan's Church**
Although not a film site—and not actually part of Aberdour Castle—the bell tower of St. Fillan's church is seen on screen at least twice, and the church is a lovely place to visit if you have the time.

"It seems likely that parts of St Fillan's church date back to at least 1123, possibly even predating neighboring Aberdour Castle … The original church comprised just the nave and chancel. The north wall of today's church and much of the chancel are likely have been part of this first structure. …

"In 1790 St Fillan's Church fell into disuse and by 1796 was a roofless ruin. …

"The church today is far from a ruin, and now serves the Aberdour parish again. This is due to the vision and commitment of local people who raised the funding needed to start restoration in 1925. … St Fillan's held its first service in well over a hundred years on 7 July 1926: and in 1973 it celebrated its 850th anniversary."

http://undiscoveredscotland.co.uk/aberdour/stfillans/

[©2015 Aberdour Festival]

**Aberdour Festival**
If you'll be visiting in late July/early August, consider attending the annual Aberdour Festival—a spectacular 10-day event featuring music and art, sport and family activities.
http://aberdourfestival.org
https://facebook.com/aberdourfestival

Outlanderites wishing to avoid crowds should go to the Aberdour Festival website and learn what dates *not* to visit Aberdour.

# Aberdour Castle: Site #3

## Learn More About Aberdour Castle:
- https://en.wikipedia.org/wiki/Aberdour_Castle
- https://en.wikipedia.org/wiki/Aberdour
- http://www.undiscoveredscotland.co.uk/aberdour/aberdourcastle/index.html
- http://www.scottishchurches.org.uk/sites/site/id/2142/name/
  St.+Fillan's+Parish+Church+Aberdour+%28Dunfermline%29+Fife

To see additional photos of "the Abbey of Ste. Anne de Beaupré," go to the **Aberdour Castle** board on our **Outlandish Scotland Journey Pinterest Site**:
https://www.pinterest.com/chasOSJ/aberdour-castle/

## OutlanderLinks

All website addresses and coordinates found in this chapter (including those in the Time & Travel section, below) are available in the **Site #3 OutlanderLinks** PDF, posted free of charge on the **Part 1 OutlanderLinks** directory of our website.
http://OutlandishScotland.com/03OutlanderLinks.pdf

    Updated information available after *Outlandish Scotland Journey* is published will also be posted in this directory.

# Time & Travel: Aberdour Castle

## Visiting Time

We suggest scheduling at least **2 hours** at Aberdour Castle—preferably **3 hours**.
- **1 hour:** A quick visit of just the film sites can be accomplished in one hour, though that allows little time in the gift shop and you'll miss all the other marvelous Aberdour Castle aspects.
- **2 hours:** Add another hour to enjoy all portions of the castle and its ruins, *or* the gardens and doocot.
- **3 hours:** To do both.
- **4 hours:** Add one more hour to visit St. Fillan's church and its 16th-century graveyard.

## Hours of Operation
- April 1st–September 30th: open daily from 9:30am to 5:30pm (last entry 5pm).
- October: open daily from 10am to 4pm (last entry 3:30pm).
- November 1st–March 31st: open daily (except for Thursdays & Fridays) from 10am to 4pm (last entry 3:30pm).
- Closed December 25th and 26th, January 1st and 2nd.
- The Gift Shop closes at last entry time.
- The Café is open April 1st–September 30th: daily, from 10:30am to 4:30pm. A self-service hot drinks machine is available the rest of the year.
- Guided tours once available in the summer were discontinued in 2014, when Aberdour Castle staffing was decreased to only one person. *Outlander*-generated increased visitor activity, however, may prompt hiring of additional staff and the return of guided tours in future. Call the castle and ask about them before you embark on your holiday—you may want to schedule extra time here if a guided tour is offered.

# Outlandish Scotland Journey: Part One

## Aberdour Castle Admission Fees
- Managed by Historic Scotland, Aberdour Castle entry is free for Explorer Pass and Scottish Heritage Pass holders. See our **Free Entry Passes** PDF for more info.
  http://OutlandishScotland.com/FreeEntryPasses.pdf
- Adults £6, Concession (seniors and unemployed with ID) £4.80,
  Child 5-15 y/o £3.30, Child under 5 free.

## Accessibility
- The upper floors of Aberdour Castle are not suitable for visitors using wheelchairs or those with limited mobility, as access is by turnpike stairs: a circular flight of steps composed of treads winding around a central pole.
- Gravel paths to the grounds can be difficult for visitors using wheelchairs, however access is possible with assistance.
- The nearest accessible toilet is at Aberdour Railway station, about 500m away.
- For additional access information, visit the link below.
  historicenvironment.scot/visit-a-place/places/aberdour-castle-and-gardens/access/

## St. Fillan's Church and Churchyard Hours of Operation
- Open every day of the year during daylight hours.
  If you visit, find the donation box and feed it, generously, please.
- Sunday services: 10:30am
  https://www.scotlandschurchestrust.org.uk/church/st-fillans-aberdour

**Please Note:** There is no parking area in or nearby St. Fillan's churchyard. Use the village car park—the same car park used for Aberdour Castle parking.

To walk from Aberdour Castle to St. Fillan's churchyard, ask a castle staff member if someone is available to let you through the gate to the churchyard from the castle's walled garden. (The gate is kept locked to control castle grounds access.) If no one is available, staff can direct you to the pedestrian/bike path that leads to the church.

## Public Transportation Directions
Take a train to Aberdour railway station [AUR].
  ScotRail Aberdour Station info:
    https://scotrail.co.uk/plan-your-journey/stations-and-facilities/aur

Alternatively, use Traveline Scotland to plan your journey.
www.travelinescotland.com
www.travelinescotland.com/apps

## Driving Directions
**The Village Car Park Coordinates:** 56.054190, -3.301037
Located at Aberdour's railway station, this car park is free and only a short walk (3 minutes) from the castle. Parking at the castle is limited, and should only be used by those with mobility difficulties.

**Aberdour Castle Courtyard:** 56.055470, -3.297699
This is where you'll enter the Admission Office/Gift Shop and gain access to the castle and its grounds. (The limited parking is here.)

# Dysart Harbor: Site #4

*Outlander* Season Two Film Site
The French Port of Le Havre

[©2009 Dysart Trust segment (enhanced)]

Dysart ("DYE-zart") is a small, 13th century town that became a royal burgh in the late 15th century. Located on the southeastern coast of Scotland, between Kirkcaldy and West Wemyss in the county of Fife, Dysart is now considered a suburb of Kirkcaldy.

"Dysart was recorded as a port as early as 1450 with an export trade in salt and coal … There was no harbour as such at the time, with the ships being grounded in the bay at Pan Ha' and loaded when the tide was out. … The build of Dysart harbour was started in the early seventeenth century, raising the east pier by building on existing reefs of rock running in a southerly direction. The inner harbour was constructed on the site of a former quarry, and the chisel marks of the quarry workers can still be seen on the steep rock face above it."
http://www.dysart-trust.org.uk/ourtrust/ourtrust.htm

Thanks to decades of conservation efforts on the part of several organizations—including the National Trust for Scotland and Historic Scotland—Dysart's harbor has been preserved for posterity, as have many of the town's historically significant landmark buildings.

# Outlandish Scotland Journey: Part One

[©2005 Robert A. Dalgleish]

In May and June of 2015, *Outlander* Season Two filming took place in the harbor. "Dysart will portray the French port of Le Havre in the 1740s."
thecourier.co.uk/news/local/fife/outlander-clipper-pulls-in-crowds-at-dysart-harbour

[©2015 ScotlandNow.DailyRecord.co.uk segments (enhanced)]

While only a few set structures were constructed on site for filming, a considerable collection of props and set-dressing elements were brought in. Additionally, several green screens were erected to facilitate a substantial amount of Computer-Generated Imagery (CGI) embellishments in post production. Basically, only the bare bones of what is seen on screen can be found in the real-world.

[Season Two Promo Pic]  [*Outlander* Season 2 screenshot] Segments, enhanced.

The steeply chiseled face of the old rock quarry that dominates the Dysart Harbor landscape can be recognized in the background of some Le Havre scenes, as seen above, left. In most footage shot here, however, the rock face was covered with CGI-created medieval French harbor buildings.

# Dysart Harbor: Site #4

[Internet-posted pic, ©Unknown]  [*Outlander* Season 2 screenshot] Segments, enhanced.

Outlanderites armed with the screenshot above will recognize that the harbor-side of the Harbourmaster's House was seen onscreen—although window shutters and stairs leading to an enclosed (faux) entry were added.

Dysart Harbor receives a **Might-Be-Fun** rating because:
- Dysart Harbor looks very little like what was seen on screen. Most Outlanderites will be happier spending their holiday time at more recognizable film sites.
- Outlanderites with an abundance of holiday time, however, may enjoy strolling through the harbor—possibly also walking to the other historic landmark buildings in Dysart.
- Why not a **Skip It** rating? Stopping at the Dysart Harbor film site while enroute from Aberdour Castle (Site #3) to Balgonie Castle (Site #5) will add only 20 minutes to your drive. If you limit your visit to 30 minutes at the film site, Dysart adds only one hour to an Outlandish Scotland Journey itinerary.

## Other Dysart Places of Interest

[©2009 kilnburn]

The Harbourmaster's House on Hot Pot Wynd (wynd rhymes with "kind") is an 18th century building originally used to store incoming cargo. It later became the home of

# Outlandish Scotland Journey: Part One

Dysart's Harbourmaster. Restored in 2006 as part of a £1 million project, the building now houses the Fife Coast and Countryside Trust headquarters—an environmental charity responsible for managing, developing and promoting elements of Fife's coast and countryside.

Being the very first coastal centre constructed in Fife, the Harbourmaster's House also has a small Dysart museum. Here, you'll find interactive displays demonstrating the region's history, its relationship to the North Sea, and the ancient trading routes between European ports and Dysart.

Dysart's Harbourmaster's House also offers public toilets and a lovely café. Because it lies between the Dysart Harbor car park and the *Outlander* film site, you'll certainly want to pop in during your visit—if only to use the loo.

**Hours of Operation**
- March–October: 9:30am to 4:30pm, 7 days a week.
- November–February: 10am to 3:30 pm, 7 days a week.
- Closed on Christmas and New Years day.

www.fifecoastalpath.co.uk/plan-your-trip/harbourmaster-s-house.aspx

[©2009 kilnburn] [©2010 kilnburn] Segments, enhanced.

Just east of the harbor car park are the ruins of St. Serf's Church (seen in the background, above, left). Built early in the 16th century, its landmark tower was added at a later date. You can wander St. Serf's old graveyard between dawn and dusk on any day of the year.

> "The cemetery contains many fine examples of table tomb stones with symbols of the trades and occupations of the people interred there.
>
> "If you manage to climb the 103 steps of the newel, or turnpike stair of the Tower, you emerge on to the parapet with its cap house. This contains a large fireplace and would have been used by the guards who kept a lookout for the marauding English. The views from the top on a clear day are spectacular and well worth the climb."

http://www.dysart-trust.org.uk/stserf/stserf.htm

St. Serf's tower overlooks the Pan Ha' stone houses (also above, left) that were built in the 18th century to replace the row of wood and turf huts that had previously sheltered fishers, colliers (coal workers), and salters. Restored in the late 1960s, these houses now are private dwellings. Happily, the residents are accustomed to tourists strolling down Pan Ha' lane and snapping pix.

http://www.dysart-trust.org.uk/panha/ph-history.htm

# Dysart Harbor: Site #4

If you venture into the village, you'll be able to see the Dysart Tolbooth (above, right) built in 1576, and the adjacent Town Hall which was built in 1887. Operated by the Dysart Trust—a small group of volunteers—these buildings are only occasionally open to the public. Access on other dates may be possible if you contact the trust while planning your visit and request a special tour appointment.
http://www.dysart-trust.org.uk/ourtrust/ourtrust.htm

## Outlandish Extra Info

[©2015 ScotlandNow.DailyRecord.co.uk]   [©2011 Nilfanion] Segments, enhanced.

Alas, it is entirely unlikely that an 18th Century Brigantine will be docked in Dysart Harbor when you visit. But, we thought you might enjoy learning more about the **Phoenix**—the ship that appeared on screen in both Seasons One and Two of *Outlander*. The information below is from the website of the company that owns her.
- The Phoenix was built in Frederikshavn, Denmark in 1929.
- She began her working life as an evangelical Mission Schooner. Twenty years later she retired from missionary work and carried cargo until her engine room was damaged by fire.
- She was bought by new owners in 1974 who converted her into a Brigantine.
- Purchased by Square Sail in Miami in 1987; a first aid over-haul enabled her to sail back to the UK where she underwent a complete refit.
- In 1991 she was converted to the 15th century Caravel **Santa Maria** for Ridley Scott's film *1492: Conquest of Paradise*.
- The ship was known as Santa Maria until 1996 when, due to increasing demand for period square-riggers, she was converted into the two-masted 18th Century Brig she is today, and reverted to her original name, **Phoenix of Dell Quay**.
    http://www.square-sail.com/

The *Phoenix*'s other film credits include:
- *Hornblower* (*Horatio Hornblower* in the USA)
- *Voyage of Discovery*
- *Frenchman's Creek*
- *The Scarlet Pimpernel*
- *Voyage of the Dawn Treader*
- *In the Heart of the Sea*

https://en.wikipedia.org/wiki/Phoenix_%281929_ship%29

# Outlandish Scotland Journey: Part One

[*Outlander* Season 1 *To Ransom a Man's Soul* screenshot segments (enhanced)]

In the last episode of *Outlander* Season One, the Phoenix played the **Cristabel**—the ship that bore Claire and Jamie to France. Season Two scenes shot in Dysart were of the Cristabel's arrival in the port of Le Havre.

## Learn More About Dysart:
- http://undiscoveredscotland.co.uk/kirkcaldy/dysart/
- https://en.wikipedia.org/wiki/Dysart,_Fife
- http://www.visitscotland.com/en-us/info/see-do/harbourmasters-house-p256031

To see additional photos of "Le Havre" and the Dysart film site, go to the **Dysart Harbor** board on our **Outlandish Scotland Journey Pinterest Site**:
https://www.pinterest.com/chasOSJ/dysart-harbor/

## OutlanderLinks

All website addresses and coordinates found in this chapter (including those in the Time & Travel section, below) are available in the **Site #4 OutlanderLinks** PDF, posted free of charge on the **Part 1 OutlanderLinks** directory of our website.
http://OutlandishScotland.com/04OutlanderLinks.pdf

Updated Dysart Harbor information available after *Outlandish Scotland Journey* is published will also be posted in this directory.

# Time & Travel: Dysart Harbor

## Visiting Time

**30 minutes** ought to be sufficient to park, dash to the harbor and snap a few pix of where Le Havre port scenes were shot. If you want to spend time in the Harbourmaster's House (visiting the shop, museum, or café)—or walk to other places of interest in Dysart—add additional time.

# Dysart Harbor: Site #4

## Dysart Harbor Location Coordinates
- The Harbourmaster's House: 56.123318, -3.123888
- St. Serf's Tower and Church Graveyard: 56.124184, -3.121958
    (When at the Harbourmaster's House, ask directions to the graveyard's entrance.)
- The Pan Ha' Houses: 56.123747, -3.122194
- Dysart's Tolbooth and Town Hall: 56.126053, -3.121139

## Outlandish Scotland Journey Dysart Map
Outlanderites who journey to Dysart solely to visit the film site will have no need of a map. The Harbourmaster's House can be seen from the car park. The Season Two Le Havre harbor film site is just beyond it.

To assist those who also wish to visit other sites in Dysart, we created a map identifying all the places listed above, and posted it on our website's **Part 1 OutlanderLinks** directory. http://OutlandishScotland.com/04DysartMap.pdf

## Public Transportation Directions
If using public transportation to accomplish your Outlandish Scotland Journey, *SKIP* Dysart. It's simply not worth the time and trouble to visit this film site if you're not driving.

## Driving Directions
**Dysart Harbor Car Park Coordinates:** 56.123373, -3.123325

# Balgonie Castle: Site #5

*Outlander* Season One Film Site
MacRannoch's Eldridge Manor

[©2014 Susanne www.adventuresaroundscotland.com/ segment (enhanced)]

Situated on land owned by the Sibbald family as early as 1246, the oldest portions of Balgonie Castle—its fortified courtyard and tower house (keep)—date from the 14th Century. Late in the 15th century, the property and castle passed to the Lundie family through a Sibbald heiress.

In 1496, Sir Robert Lundie built a two-storey range of buildings to the east of the keep that included a long hall and solar.

"This range incorporated an earlier corner tower and the 14th-century chapel. King James IV visited Balgonie on 20 August 1496, and gave 18 shillings to the masons as a gift."
https://en.wikipedia.org/wiki/Balgonie_Castle

Between the 15th and 18th centuries, the castle was inherited or purchased by several other families, many of whom added to what came before. It wasn't until the 19th century that the castle came close to being lost.

"In 1824 the castle was sold to James Balfour of Whittingehame … He was unable to arrest the decay which was advancing, and in the mid nineteenth century the roofs were removed to avoid paying tax on the property. Much vandalism occurred in the 1960s, and it was not until 1971 that restoration of the castle, then owned by

# Balgonie Castle: Site #5

David Maxwell, began. Work continued through the 1970s and 1980s, aided by European funding as part of European Architectural Heritage Year, in 1975. The keep and chapel have now been fully restored, and the castle is once again lived in by its current owner and laird, Raymond Morris, and his family."
https://en.wikipedia.org/wiki/Balgonie_Castle

"The present Laird of Balgonie has beautifully restored a great part of the castle, and will treat the visitor to a most interesting tour of the property. Raymond Morris is also a retired heraldic painter and wood carver, and examples of his work can be admired all through the castle. A group of rescued pet deer hounds complement this atmosphere of times gone by."
http://www.marie-stuart.co.uk/Castles/Balgonie.htm

In August of 2014, a deluge of *Outlander* construction crew and set-dressers descended on Balgonie Castle to transform it into Sir Marcus MacRannoch's Eldridge Manor for Season One episode 15 filming.

On screen and in the novel, MacRannoch's home is where Claire was taken after being tossed out of Wentworth Prison by Black Jack Randall. In the novel, Jamie also was brought to Eldridge Manor after being rescued from Wentworth, and this is where Claire repaired his hand before they journeyed to the Abbey of Ste. Anne de Beaupré in France.

[©2014 Stuart Morris of Balgonie]

For *Outlander* filming, Balgonie Castle's Lundie Hall was transformed into Eldridge Hall. Above is a photo of the hall dressed and ready to shoot. Below are two screenshots from footage filmed in the hall.

# Outlandish Scotland Journey: Part One

[*Outlander* Season 1 screenshot segments (enhanced)]

[©2014 Susanne at AdventuresAroundScotland.com (enhanced)]

In reality, the Lundie Hall is often either empty or set up for a wedding reception.

[©2014 Stuart Morris of Balgonie segments (enhanced)]

Balgonie Castle's courtyard was augmented with an amazing amount of set dressing elements before filming, especially considering the fact that *none* of these Outlandish details were ever visible on screen—not even for a fleeting moment.

# Balgonie Castle: Site #5

[*Outlander* Season 1 screenshot (enhanced)]

All exterior Eldridge Manor scenes were shot at night, while the courtyard was swarming with shaggy highland "coos" (cows). [BTW: The door seen behind Murtagh in the screenshot above can be found beneath the balcony seen in the real-world photo below.]

[©2014 Susanne at AdventuresAroundScotland.com segment (enhanced)]

Balgonie Castle currently has a **Skip-It** rating because it was closed to the public in February of 2019, "due to the health and age of the Laird." Should it reopen in the future, we will post a notice on the **Part 1 OutlanderLinks** directory of our website.

When open, Balgonie Castle receives a **Might-Be-Fun** rating because:
- With all the terrifically detailed set dressing elements long gone, Balgonie's Lundie Hall looks very little like what was seen on screen. Outlanderites with limited holiday time will be happier spending it at more recognizable film sites.

# Outlandish Scotland Journey: Part One

- Why not a **Skip It** rating?
    **Reason #1:** This is an absolutely marvelous place to visit! Balgonie's Laird is a gracious host–as is his son–who thoroughly enjoys regaling Outlanderites with tales of the filming that took place there. Additionally, rumor has it that a few Eldridge Manor props were left behind for Balgonie Castle visitors to enjoy.
    **Reason #2:** Stopping at Balgonie Castle while enroute to **Falkland Village (Site #6)** from **Aberdour Castle (Site #3)**—*or* from **Dysart Harbor (Site #4)**—only adds 12 minutes to your drive. If your itinerary can afford an additional hour (or two) spent at Balgonie Castle, you'll not be disappointed.

## Learn More About Balgonie Castle:
- http://www.balgoniecastletours.co.uk/
- https://www.facebook.com/toursbalgonie/
- http://www.adventuresaroundscotland.com/travel-blog/six-must-visit-locations-in-fife-for-outlander-fans
- http://www.tripadvisor.com/Attraction_Review-g1065827-d7051762-Reviews-Balgonie_Castle-Markinch_Glenrothes_Fife_Scotland.html

Additional photos found on the Internet are available in the **Balgonie Castle** board of our **Outlandish Scotland Journey Pinterest Site**:
https://www.pinterest.com/chasOSJ/balgonie-castle/

## OutlanderLinks
All website addresses and coordinates found in this chapter (including those in the Time & Travel section, below) are available in the **Site #5 OutlanderLinks** PDF, posted free of charge on the **Part 1 OutlanderLinks** directory of our website.
http://OutlandishScotland.com/05OutlanderLinks.pdf
    Updated Balgonie Castle information available after *Outlandish Scotland Journey* is published will also be posted in this directory.

# Time & Travel: Balgonie Castle
## Visiting Time
A minimum of 1 hour—2 or more hours if you'll be arranging for a private tour.

## Hours of Operation & Admission Fees
When it reopens, we will post this information on the **Part 1 OutlanderLinks** directory of our website.

## Balgonie Castle Car Park Coordinates
These also will be posted when the castle reopens.

# Falkland Village: Site #6

## Film Site for *Outlander* Seasons One, Two, and Four
## Inverness in 1945, 1746, 1968, and 1971!

Falkland is a wonderful wee village in the county of Fife that dates back to the Middle Ages and has a strong Jacobite connection. Falkland Palace was one of Mary Queen of Scots' favorite country residences. Her great grandson, King James II of England (James VII of Scotland)—grandfather of Charles Edward Stuart—declared the village a Royal Burgh in 1458.

[©2013 STARZ Entertainment]

## Outlander Season One Filming in Falkland Village

It was Ron Moore's decision to film 1945 Inverness scenes—scenes of Frank and Claire Randal enjoying a second honeymoon—in Falkland, for *Outlander* Season One, Episode 1, *Sassenach*, scenes.

"There are several buildings and streets [here] that felt the most like they would play 1940s," says Moore. "There's not a lot of signage. It's pretty much how you see it in the show and pretty much how you want a Scottish village to be in your

# Outlandish Scotland Journey: Part One

mind's eye. It's a great place to actually visit: very friendly, easy to access, great for walking around, pubs, restaurants."
http://www.cntraveler.com/galleries/2015-03-25/outlander-in-scotland-with-ron-moore-sam-heughan

Falkland's fabulous state of preservation is largely due to its 1970 designation as Scotland's first conservation area.
"There are few other villages in the country quite so rich in awesome old buildings. The quaint old houses, the narrow streets with cobbled pavements (sidewalks) … all take me back into history. There is an exhibition on the history of the Falkland Palace and the Burgh in the restored town hall which was bought in 1986 by [the National Trust for Scotland], which has also been responsible for restoring so many of the 'little houses' in the town."
http://www.scotlands-enchanting-kingdom.com/history-of-falkland-palace.html

[*Outlander* Season 1 screenshot segment (enhanced)]

The first footage filmed for the *Outlander* TV series was shot in Falkland on October 16th, 2013—making this a landmark film site. All exterior 1945 Inverness scenes for Episode 1 were filmed in the area of Falkland Village's Old Market Square, situated around the Bruce Fountain and Market Cross.

[*Outlander* Season 1 screenshot segment (enhanced)]

# Falkland Village: Site #6

The first Falkland location seen on screen is the window of Farrells General Store, where Claire admires the vases on display and reflects on the pros and cons of her nomadic life.

[©2013 STARZ Entertainment]  [©2015 jillyjillyblog.co.uk] Segments, enhanced.

In 2013, Fayre Earth gift shop owner *Elizabeth* Adams allowed *Outlander* filmmakers to transform her storefront into that of Farrells General Store. The paint scheme was altered to create a 1940s look, a window box with display racks was installed, and the cobbled sidewalk was covered with concrete-like blocks.

The Fayre Earth gift shop sells "locally made, recycled and fairly traded" products, and is also a coffeehouse.
**Opening Hours:** 10am to 5pm, 7 days a week. facebook.com/FayreEarthGiftShop/

[©2013 Amber Linfield Photography]  [Internet-posted pic ©Unknown] Segments, enhanced.

Campbell's Café—a place not mentioned in the novel—is seen in the background of several *Outlander* Episode 1 scenes (photo above, left). Although many Internet sources report Lomond Pharmacy as being the business operating in this building at the time of filming, the pharmacy had moved to a new location nine months earlier, in February of 2013.

Campbell's Coffeehouse & Eatery (photo above, right) opened here in September of 2013, shortly before set dressers arrived in the village—hence, the name of the café seen on screen.

As with the transformation of Fayre Earth's storefront, filmmakers dramatically changed the café's paint scheme. To hide the real-world Campbell's modern interior, they installed window boxes, curtains, and covered the glass doors. The sidewalk needed no alteration, apart from removing the accessibility ramp.

**Opening Hours:** 10am to 5pm, daily. campbellscoffeehouse.com/

# Outlandish Scotland Journey: Part One

[©2013 Amber Linfield Photography] [©2014 Nicola Holland] Segments, enhanced.

Next door to Campbell's is a secondhand violin and antique shop owned and operated by Robert (Bob) Beveridge (photo above, right). This storefront was altered only by painting the white window trim black, and mounting a business sign that read, "H. Allingham Music." The hanging violins and sign seen in the shop window are real-world features. Thus, this business looks almost exactly as it did when seen—albeit fleetingly—on screen.

Lucky Outlanderites who stop in may be treated to Bob playing a tune on the guitar given him by Roseanne Cash when she visited Falkland shortly after her father's death in 2003. Years before, Johnny Cash had traced his family's roots back to Fife and visited the village several times. During his last trip to Falkland in 1981, Bob was the person who looked after Cash and his friend, Andy Williams.
www.theguardian.com/music/2010/feb/07/johnny-cash-scottish-roots
https://tjrossjoiners.wordpress.com/tag/strathmiglo-fife/

Even luckier Outlanderites may get Bob to tell them about other aspects of his interesting personal history.

"Only on persuasion did we learn of his career with the police homicide squad in Glasgow. Also we heard of his carrying an unexploded WW2 bomb from a children's walk [in Falkland] to a disposal point."
http://www.information-britain.co.uk/reviews.php?place=25770&type=2

[*Outlander* Season 1 screenshot segment (enhanced)]

Next we come to Mrs. Baird's Bed & Breakfast, which also borders the Old Market Square in Falkland—as seen in the screenshots above and below.

# Falkland Village: Site #6

In the novel, the blood of a black cockerel was sprinkled on the doorstep of Mrs. Baird's B&B, as well as doorsteps of other nearby residences. Mrs. Baird explained that this practice was a time-honored tradition performed prior to the Gaelic spring festival of Beltane — aka May Day.

[*Outlander* Season 1 screenshot (enhanced)]

For filming the TV series, however, the overhead lintel and door frames of Mrs. Baird's and surrounding residences were dramatically drizzled with (faux) black cockerel's blood, to assuage the ghosts believed to accompany the upcoming Gaelic fall festival of Samhain — aka, Halloween. Clearly, a little doorstep sprinkle wasn't enough of a visual statement for a television show.

[©2015 Kimberly Kahl]  [Internet-posted pic ©Unknown] Segments, enhanced.

In reality, the building used to film exterior shots of Mrs. Baird's 1945 Inverness B&B is the Covenanter Hotel. Little more than hanging a different sign and repainting the columns and window trim was required to transform the hotel's exterior for 2013 *Outlander* filming. And, yes, you can lodge here!

"We offer a choice of three bedrooms and a self catering apartment; all have been newly refurbished to a high standard … with views overlooking Falkland square.
… Wake up to a full Scottish breakfast before setting off for the day.

# Outlandish Scotland Journey: Part One

> "The Hotel's restaurant is a coffee shop during the day and a Bistro/Restaurant in the evening with a carvery available on Sunday. ... There is an all-day menu which offers an excellent choice of dishes ... Also delightful sweets and various coffees and teas available. There is also a quaint wine bar to relax and enjoy a various selection of wines, beers and spirits."
> http://www.covenanterfalkland.co.uk/

Unfortunately, you cannot lodge in the same room that Claire and Frank did when visiting Inverness in 1945. Scenes in that room were shot within **Hunterston House**, a film site featured in our **Not Going to Go There** Outlandish Extra PDF.
www.OutlandishScotland.com/NotGoingThere.pdf

If you book far enough in advance, however, you may be able to stay in the Covenanter Hotel room with the window featured in the iconic screenshot of Jamie watching Claire brush her hair while standing by the fountain. Ask about it when you call them to book your room.

[*Outlander* Season 4 screenshot segment (enhanced)]

Falkland's Market Square and "Baird's Bed and Breakfast" (now run by *Miss* Baird) appear on screen one last time in *Outlander*—Episode 5 of Season Four. Filmed in January of 2018, these scenes take place in 1971, when Roger is tracking Brianna.

At last we come to the iconic Bruce Fountain that stands in the center of Falkland Village's Old Market Square. Here is where rain-drenched night scenes were shot of Jamie's "ghost" watching Claire through the window of Mrs. Baird's B&B.

Outlanderites the world over are still waiting to learn how—and from *when*—Jamie's spirit arrived in 1945 Inverness. However! Because the answer won't be revealed until Diana Gabaldon publishes her final *Outlander* series novel (book 10), we're not all that eager to know.

# Falkland Village: Site #6

[*Outlander* Season 1 screenshot (enhanced)]

Nothing about the Bruce Fountain was altered for filming. Since the real-world fountain's *octagonally*-spired topper is illuminated at night, you may be able to snap nighttime shots here—if you have the right equipment—as well as daytime pix.

[©2014 Susanne at AdventuresAroundScotland.com (enhanced)]

**FYI:** Falkland's Bruce Fountain has absolutely nothing to do with Robert the Bruce of Scottish history and *Braveheart* fame. (Robert the Bruce was born in 1274, and died in 1329.)

Falkland's Bruce Fountain was commissioned in 1853 by a man originally named Onesiphorus Tyndall—a man commonly regarded as an "impecunious barrister."

In 1828, Onesiphorus married a local Falkland heiress, Margaret Steuart [sic] Hamilton Bruce. Upon their marriage he adopted his wife's surname, and became Onesiphorus

# Outlandish Scotland Journey: Part One

Tyndall Bruce. Soon thereafter, his new wife paid off all of the exorbitant debts he had accrued prior to their marriage.

Happily, the couple managed Margaret's inherited properties quite well after their marriage, improving and extending them. By significantly contributing to the village, they also eventually earned the approval of Falkland folk.

> "They paid for the building of the present Falkland Parish church, and Onesiphorus was commemorated by a prominent monument on the Lomond Hills ... as well as by this statue next to the church. Both Onesiphorus and Margaret are buried in the parish kirkyard."
> http://www.geograph.org.uk/photo/2536211

Two of the four red lions perched on the corners of Falkland's Bruce Fountain hold shields bearing the Tyndall-Bruce Arms, while the other two hold shields sporting the Royal Burgh of Falkland's symbol.

## Outlander Season Two Filming in Falkland Village
## Part One

In December of 2015 we were thrilled to learn that additional filming would take place in Falkland for *Outlander* Season Two. Given the previous scenes shot here—and the content of Diana's second novel, *Dragonfly in Amber*—we anticipated that the Season Two scenes would be those that took place in *1948* Inverness, when Claire traveled back to the future and returned to Frank. We were wrong!

[©2016 Brian Milne segments (enhanced)]

On January 21st, 2016, Falkland again doubled as Inverness, but in *1746*—on the days just prior to the battle of Culloden.

# Falkland Village: Site #6

[Google Street View image segment (enhanced)]

To reach the first 1746 film site, walk south of the Bruce Fountain, along Cross Wynd (between the Covenanter Hotel and the Fayre Earth gift shop). Within a short block, you'll reach Brunton Street.

Turn right and—voila!—you've arrived at the film site for the first exterior 1746 Inverness street scenes seen in Season Two's Episode 12, *The Hail Mary*.

[Google Street View image]   [©2016 Robbie Nellies] Segments, enhanced.

As you can see in the film site photo above right, the little park on the north side of Brunton Street was filled with support tents during 2016 filming. The street itself—as well as the exterior of all buildings lining its south side—was considerably transformed, so as to represent a 17th century street.

Brunton Street plays two different locations in 1746 Inverness, the most important one being the lane where Black Jack Randall procured lodgings for his ailing brother, Alex.

Outlanderites who've read the *Dragonfly In Amber* novel will know that Alex's last lodgings actually were located on Lady Walk Wynd—a fictional lane in **Edinburgh (Site #38)**. On screen, however, the events that culminated in Mary Hawkins' marriage took place in an Inverness boarding house.

We first see Brunton Street as Claire enters from its western end (screenshot below), walking east and passing between Rotten Row (to the north) and Sharp's Close (to the south). It is April 13th, 1776—three days before the battle of Culloden, unless she and Jamie can stop it. Claire is on her way to an Inverness apothecary shop to replenish her medical supplies, but we do not see her actually entering the shop.

# Outlandish Scotland Journey: Part One

[*Outlander* Season 2 screenshot segment (enhanced)]

Inside the shop, Clair runs into Mary Hawkins and learns of Alex's alarming state of ill heath. The interior Inverness apothecary scenes were shot in the old kitchen and bakehouse of Falkland Palace. We'll show you that film site in an upcoming section.

[*Outlander* Season 2 screenshots (enhanced)]

When next we see Brunton Street, Claire again is walking east from its western end, but this time she is headed to Alex Randall's Inverness lodgings. In the screenshot above left, Claire is looking up at the McGilvrey's Boarding House sign. This shot is followed by a close-up of the boarding house's sign—seen above, right.

Oddly enough, that is *not* the sign that was hanging on Brunton Street during filming. In fact, apart from its brief close-up, that sign never again appeared on screen.

[*Outlander* Season 2 screenshot segment (enhanced)]

# Falkland Village: Site #6

Instead—as seen in the screenshots above and below (as well as in the Robbie Nellies' Falkland filming day pic at the beginning of this section)—the McGilvrey's Boarding House sign that was mounted on a Brunton Street building contained only the graphic images of a crescent Man-in-the-Moon and a star.

[*Outlander* Season 2 screenshot segment (enhanced)]

[Starz network *Outlander* set design art]   [*Outlander* Season 2 screenshot segment (enhanced)]

Yes. We realize that this is somewhat of a moot point, since all Outlander set dressing elements are long gone and you'll not be seeing them. It's simply a conundrum we noticed, and decided to include it here for your edification.

> **BTW:** Boarding house interior scenes were shot on a sound stage set at Cumbernauld's Wardpark Studios, as were interior Inverness tavern scenes.

When you visit, you'll see that the building at the west end of Brunton Street has a white harled plaster exterior. This building was painted a dull brown for 2016 Season Two filming. (See the pix below.)

Brunton Street ends where it meets a tiny lane leading south—Sharps Close.
> **"Sharps Close is a typical ancient Wynd,** narrow and cobbled, with single storey weavers' cottages stepped up the slope. All of Falkland's streets were once cobbled like this."
> http://www.explore-st-andrews.com/areas/east-fife/falkland/

# Outlandish Scotland Journey: Part One

[Google Street View image] [©2016 OutlanderTVnews.com] Segments, enhanced.

As you can see in the film set pic above right, Sharps Close was also well dressed prior to January of 2016 *Outlander* filming. Particular attention was paid to removing all evidence of the Cottage Craft Centre still operating on its northwest corner, including replacement of the centre's modern door and windowpanes with 17th century versions.
https://www.tripadvisor.com/Attraction_Review-g551747-d13401105-Reviews-The_Cottage_Craft-Falkland_Fife_Scotland.html

[*Outlander* Season 2 screenshots (enhanced)]

It was at the Brunton Street mouth of Sharps Close that two important confrontation scenes were filmed for *The Hail Mary*. (That's Sharps Close in the background between Murtagh and Claire, above right.)

[Google Street View image segment (enhanced)]

Directly northwest of where Sharps Close meets Brunton Street is another little lane—Rotten Row. Normally barricaded to prevent thru traffic, Rotten Row also is a 1746 Inverness film site.

# Falkland Village: Site #6

[©2016 OutlanderTVnews.com] [©2016 Howe Crafti] Segments, enhanced.

In addition to removing the iron traffic barriers at its southern end, Rotten Row was significantly dressed for filming.

[*Outlander* Season 2 screenshot (enhanced)]

When heading north down Rotten Row from Brunton Street and Sharps close, you'll be walking in the footsteps of Claire and Murtagh, as he escorted her to the tavern meeting with Black Jack Randall. (Based on the sign, it was probably called "White Castle Tavern.")

[Google Street View image segment (enhanced)]

# Outlandish Scotland Journey: Part One

After reaching the northern end of Rotten Row, you'll be back at the Falkland Village High Street. Turn right and return to the Old Market Square.

**BTW:** At the far left of the pic above you can see the steepled clock tower that crowns Falkland Village's Old Town Hall in the distance. Remember this!

## Outlander Season Two Filming in Falkland Village
## Part Two

In February of 2016, the *Outlander* cast and crew descended upon Falkland Village's Market Square for a third time. On the 16th of February they filmed a few scenes for the Season Two finale, episode 13, "Dragonfly in Amber." Once again doubling as Inverness, this Falkland Village footage was of Claire's visit in 1968.

[*Outlander* Season 2 screenshot (enhanced)]

First, Claire is seen driving into the Inverness (Falkland Village) Old Market Square, passing what once was Farrells General store. Sometime in the past 20 years, it has become Farrells *& Son* General store. The real-world location that again was transformed into a Farrells' store is the Fayre Earth gift shop.

**1945** [©2013 STARZ] **1968** [©2016 Robbie Nellies] Segments, enhanced.

# Falkland Village: Site #6

[*Outlander* Season 2 screenshot segment (enhanced)]

After that, Claire emerges from behind the iconic Bruce Fountain, having passed what was Campbell's Café in 1945. In 1968, however, Campbell's Café has become a grocery store.

**1945** [©2013 Amber Linfield Photography] **1968** [©2016 Robbie Nellies] Segments, enhanced.

Remember that the real-world location transformed into Campbell's Café for 1945 scenes actually *is* the current-day Campbell's Café in Falkland Village. Filmmakers covered up the café entrance for 1968 Inverness footage, to create the grocery.

[*Outlander* Season 2 screenshot (enhanced)]

# Outlandish Scotland Journey: Part One

Next, Claire passes by what *still* appears to be Mrs. Baird's B&B (at center, above). It has the same paint scheme and sign as seen in 1945—though the sign is hung on the corner of the building instead of beside the door.

Seconds later, she reaches her destination: the Inverness County Records Office.

[Google Street View image segment (enhanced)]

Which, in reality, is the Falkland Village Old Town Hall, located immediately east of the Covenanter Hotel. Its tall, steepled clock tower (which we pointed out earlier) isn't seen on screen, or in the Google Streetview segment above.

## Outlander Season Two Falkland Village Filming
## Part Three: Falkland Palace

[*Outlander* Season 1 screenshot segment (enhanced)]

Falkland Palace is only half a block northeast of the Covenanter Hotel, as seen in the screenshot above. Given its close proximity to Mrs. Baird's B&B, the palace entrance often appears in the background of Season One, Episode 1, *Sassenach*, scenes.

# Falkland Village: Site #6

[©2015 Bruce & Carol Conway segment (enhanced)]

"The history of Falkland Palace can be traced back to the middle Ages, when it was home to the Earls of Fife. ... James II declared the village of Falkland a Royal Burgh [in 1458] ...

"King James IV rebuilt the original structure between 1501 and 1513 ... James V added to the buildings there, transforming it into a sophisticated Renaissance palace. He was also responsible for adding the royal tennis court in 1539 ... He died at the Palace in 1542 and his baby daughter, Mary, became Queen.

"Mary Queen of Scots was a frequent visitor, enjoying the peace and tranquility there and getting away from the problems and politics of Edinburgh. She enjoyed playing tennis, riding, hunting and hawking around Falkland. The Royal Tennis Court is reputed to be the oldest surviving Royal Tennis court of its kind in the world."
www.scotlands-enchanting-kingdom.com/history-of-falkland-palace

[©2014 Glen Bowman]

Once a royal palace of the Scottish Kings, today Falkland Palace is consigned to the stewardship of the 7th Marquess of Bute. He, however, delegates all of his duties to the

# Outlandish Scotland Journey: Part One

National Trust for Scotland—the organization that restored the salvageable sections of Falkland Palace in 1954.

> "Experience a day in the life of the Stuart monarchs at Falkland Palace, their country residence for 200 years—and a favorite place of Mary, Queen of Scots. … Part of the Palace is in ruins but the original and reconstructed rooms are packed with 17th-century Flemish tapestries, elaborate painted ceilings and antique furnishings. The beautiful, tranquil grounds are worth a visit alone. They are home to the oldest Real or Royal tennis court in Britain, built for King James V."
> https://www.nts.org.uk/visit/places/falkland-palace

To learn more about Falkland Palace, visit Undiscovered Scotland's website. There you'll also find photos of the palace's architecture, the rooms within, and the gardens.
http://www.undiscoveredscotland.co.uk/falkland/falklandpalace/

**Outlander Season Two Falkland Palace Filming**
Interior scenes of the Inverness apothecary that Claire visited in Episode 12, *The Hail Mary*, were filmed within the Falkland Palace old kitchen and bakehouse.

[Falkland Palace Virtual Tour screenshot segment (enhanced), ©The National Trust for Scotland]

[*Outlander* Season 2 screenshot (enhanced)]

Although nothing of what was seen on screen remains, you'll still enjoy stepping inside this space—especially when armed with the screenshot above.

# Falkland Village: Site #6

### Hours of Operation
- **Falkland Palace:** March 1st–October 31, Monday to Saturday 11am–5pm; Sunday noon to 5pm (last entry 4:30pm).
- **Falkland Palace Shop:** Same hours as above, in addition to
  November–January, Monday to Saturday 11am–4pm; Sunday 1–4pm
  February, Saturday to Wednesday 11am–4pm; Sunday 1–4pm
  The NTS Falkland Palace Shop is half a block east of the Falkland Palace entrance.

### Falkland Palace and Garden Admission
- Free Entry is granted to NTS Members, NTS Discover Ticket holders, and Scottish Heritage Pass holders.
- Adult: £13
- Concession (Seniors and Students with ID): £9
- Family: £30
- One Parent Family: £23.50.

### Falkland Palace Accessibility
"Falkland Palace is unsuitable for wheelchairs or anyone with mobility challenges due to the number of stairs. However, 'armchair visits' are available via the guidebook and there's access to many parts of the garden via the main entrance (some gravel paths).

"The shop is not suitable for wheelchairs—there are four steps into the shop from the street entrance.

"There's an accessible toilet at the car park in the centre of Falkland, a short walk from the palace."

https://www.nts.org.uk/visit/places/falkland-palace/planning-your-visit#accessibility-information

## Other Falkland Places of Interest

[©2013 Jessica Tivy segment (enhanced)]

# Outlandish Scotland Journey: Part One

Falkland's Parish Church occupies the north side of the Old Market Square—diagonally across from the Covenanter Hotel.

> "The first [Falkland Parish Church] was erected in 1595 after Falkland received its royal charter. It was replaced in 1620 but the building was said to be in poor condition by the 1840s, necessitating its demolition. The present church was built between 1848 and 1850 [funded by Onesiphorus Tyndall Bruce], and consists of a four bay main cell and a three stage tower."

http://www.scottishchurches.org.uk/sites/site/id/4697/name/Falkland+Parish+Church+%28present%29+Falkland+Fife

[©2015 Bruce & Carol Conway] [Internet-posted fan pic ©Unknown] Segments, enhanced.

Topped by a tall, Victorian Gothic tower, only portions of Falkland Parish Church were seen onscreen in the episode 101 scenes shot at street level. Because Frank parked in front of the church property's eastern end, however, all modern day signage was removed and a **Dalneigh Parish Church** sign was erected behind the fence, near the car.

Dalneigh Parish Church can still be found in Inverness today. Oddly enough, it wasn't built until 1953. Which means that the Dalneigh Parish Church didn't exist when Claire and Frank visited Inverness in 1945. We have absolutely no idea why *Outlander* filmmakers chose to represent this particular Inverness church on-screen—making this an interesting (though, unanswered) bit of *Outlander* TV trivia.

Falkland Parish Church is open to the public from mid-June to mid-September, Monday to Friday, 2–4pm, or by special arrangement.
https://www.scotlandschurchestrust.org.uk/church/falkland-parish-church

If you wish to attend Sunday Services, visit the website below for dates and times.
http://www.standrewspresbytery.org.uk/standrewschurches

Falkland Village: Site #6

[©2016 www.facebook.com/pages/FALKLAND-FESTIVAL (enhanced)

The Falkland Midsummer Festival—a week of "community events and family fun"—is organized and run by local residents and volunteers, funded through grants and donations. It is an annual festival, usually held in mid-to-late June.

The dates for each year's festival are posted on the festival's Facebook page.

[©2015 falklandfestival.blogspot.com segments (enhanced)]

A fabulous Street Fair is held on at least one day during the Falkland Midsummer Festival. On Street Fair day, the stalls of local artisans, crafters, food vendors—and much, much more—fill the Old Market Square and overflow down all the little lanes leading to it.

We highly recommend attending the Falkland Midsummer Festival. Unless you'll be visiting Falkland for two days, however, we strongly suggest *avoiding* the village on a Street Fair day, as you'll not be able to shoot unimpeded pix of the *Outlander* film sites during the Street Fair.

The Falkland Traditional Music Festival is another annual event held in the village. It usually is scheduled during the first weekend of July.

"The Falkland Traditional Music Festival is now in its fourth year [(2016)] and will continue with its successful programme of ceilidhs, concerts, workshops and a range of traditional music and song competitions. Opening event—a ceilidh dance on Friday 1 July. Saturday 2 July will start at 10:00 in the morning with instrumental workshops, as well as workshops on traditional song and ballad and storytelling followed by an afternoon of competitions for fiddle, accordion, traditional song, bothy ballad, instrumental pairs/duets and ceilidh bands—followed by an early evening concert with guests and prize winners."

# Outlandish Scotland Journey: Part One

[©2015 https://www.facebook.com/falklandtradfest (enhanced)]

Visit Falkland Traditional Music Festival's website to learn the dates for each year's festival.
http://falklandtradfest.org.uk/

While either of Falkland's annual festivals would be terrifically fun to attend, Outlanderites wishing to avoid large crowds should go to each festival's Facebook page to discover what dates to *not* to visit Falkland.

## Learn More About Falkland:
- https://en.wikipedia.org/wiki/Falkland,_Fife
- www.visitscotland.com/en-us/info/towns-villages/falkland-p238941
- www.undiscoveredscotland.co.uk/falkland/falkland/
- www.information-britain.co.uk/county57/townguideFalkland/
- https://en.wikipedia.org/wiki/Falkland_Palace

To see additional photos, go to the **Falkland Village** board on our **Outlandish Scotland Journey Pinterest Site**:
www.pinterest.com/chasOSJ/falkland/

## OutlanderLinks

All website addresses and coordinates found in this chapter (including those in the Time & Travel section, below) are available in the **Site #6 OutlanderLinks** PDF, posted free of charge on the **Part 1 OutlanderLinks** directory of our website.
http://OutlandishScotland.com/06OutlanderLinks.pdf

Updated Falkland Village information available after *Outlandish Scotland Journey* is published will also be posted in this directory.

Falkland Village: Site #6

# Time & Travel: Falkland Village

## Visiting Time

- **1 hour** will do if you're only interested in snapping exterior *Outlander* film site pix.
- Add **another hour** to enjoy a sip and sup at one of Falkland's cafés or pubs.
- Schedule **3–4 hours** here, if you'll also be visiting Falkland Palace and its gardens.

## Accessibility

The cobbled streets of Falkland Village may prove challenging to some, and many of the buildings have a shallow step or threshold at the entrance.

## Public Transportation Directions

Basic information for reaching Falkland via bus and train is provided on the NTS Falkland Palace and Garden webpage.
https://www.nts.org.uk/visit/places/falkland-palace/getting-here

Alternatively, use Traveline Scotland to plan your journey.
www.travelinescotland.com
www.travelinescotland.com/apps

## Driving Directions

**Falkland Village Old Market Square Coordinates:** 56.253060, -3.207938
**Falkland's Main Car Park Coordinates:** 56.252796, -3.205588

Program Falkland's Old Market Square coordinates into your vehicle's SatNav/GPS device so that you can drive through the central filming area and get the lay of the land. After that, head to the Main Car Park.

Falkland was a popular tourist destination even before the *Outlander* film site craze began, and can be quite crowded from April through September. The likelihood of finding street parking near the Old Market Square, or in the small car park behind Fayre Earth gift shop, is slim during those months. Happily, the large Falkland Village Hall and Library car park is only a 3 minute walk from the Old Market Square.

## The Outlandish Scotland Journey Falkland Map

To assist all Outlanderites visiting Falkland, we created a film sites map and posted it—free of charge—on the **Part 1 OutlanderLinks** directory of our website.
http://OutlandishScotland.com/06FalklandMap.pdf

# Outlandish Scotland Journey: Part One

[Google Map segment (enhanced)]

## Falkland Film Sites Map Key

1. **Falkland's Old Market Square:** *Outlander* Season 1, 2, and 4 Film Sites, which include:
   The Covenanter Hotel—Mrs. Baird's Bed & Breakfast
   The Iconic Bruce Fountain
   Campbell's Café—a Café in 1945, a Grocers in 1968 & 1971
   Bob Beveridge's Violin Shop—H. Allingham Music in 1945
   Fayre Earth Gift Shop—Farrells General Store
   Falkland Parish Church
2. Brunton Street—1746 film site in Season 2
3. Sharp's Close—1746 film site in Season 2
4. Rotten Row—1746 film site in Season 2
5. Falkland Old Town Hall—Inverness County Records Office in 1968
6. Falkland Palace and Gardens—Inverness apothecary in 1746
- A large Parking icon identifies the main car park at Falkland Village Hall & Library
- A small Parking icon identifies the littel car park behind Fayre Earth gift shop
- An Rx icon identifies the Lomond Pharmacy location

**Also Seen on the Map:**
- The Bank of Scotland ATM on High Street
- The Bruce Inn
- The Falkland Convenience Store (also the Post Office)
- The Hayloft Tea Room
- The Stag Inn
- The Lomond Tavern

# Falkland Village: Site #6

## Lodging in Falkland

If you'll be overnighting in Falkland, but are unable to book a room at the Covenanter Hotel, the next best place to stay is the Bruce Inn.

[Google Street View image segment (enhanced)]

Once a 15th century Royal Hunting Lodge (likely also a coaching inn), the Bruce Inn has been visited by Rob Roy and Mary Queen of Scots, as well as other Scottish Kings and Queens. Although the doorway was rebuilt in the 19th century, its ground floor windows still sport the original 15th century moldings. The crescent-shaped, engraved and painted panel mounted on the building—expressing the householder's loyalty to the King of Great Britain, France, and Ireland—is dated 1607.

Only 3 rooms are available at the Bruce Inn, but all offer tea and coffee facilities, a color TV with Freeview (the only free digital television service in the UK), and free WIFI access. The nightly room tariff includes breakfast.

The Bruce Inn's restaurant is open to the public from noon to 11pm on Mondays–Wednesdays, noon to midnight on Thursdays–Saturdays, and 12:30pm to 11pm on Sundays. Their bar, with its cozy wood-burning stove, is open every day (likely during those same hours), and occasionally offers live entertainment.
http://thebrucefalkland.co.uk/
https://www.facebook.com/TheBruceInnFalkland/

Additional Falkland area lodging suggestions (including campgrounds) can be found on the Falkland Traditional Music Festival website:
https://falklandtradfest.org.uk/accommodation/

If none of the above options fit your needs, there is a collection of Fife county guesthouse proprietors whose website is a great resource for finding a place to stay from which you can conveniently reach all of the first six Outlandish Scotland Journey sites.

> "All members of the 'A Stay in Fife' collection have been chosen for their high standards of hospitality, cleanliness and friendliness. Family owned and located throughout the county of Fife, they're some of the best bed & breakfasts on offer."
> http://astayinfife.co.uk/

If all of the above info fails to work for you, see our **Scotland Lodging Tips** PDF.
http://OutlandishScotland.com/ScotlandLodgingTips.pdf

# Tibbermore Parish Church: Site #7

## Outlander Season One Film Site
## The Cranesmuir Witchcraft Trial

Commonly called a "small village," Tibbermore Village is little more than a few houses flanking the four corners of a remote crossroad about 4 miles west of Perth, surrounded by farmland as far as the eye can see.

"Previously known as Tippermuir, [Tibbermore] was the site of the Battle of Tippermuir between the Duke of Montrose and an army of Covenanters [in 1644]."
https://en.wikipedia.org/wiki/Tibbermore

The parish of Tibbermore, however, is not at all small. It includes the villages of Tibbermore, Almondbank, and Huntingtower/Ruthvenfield, as well as a portion of the parliamentary burgh of Perth.

[©2014 Barbara Jean Lewis segment (enhanced)]

# Tibbermore Parish Church: Site #7

The old Tibbermore Parish Church is only two tenths of a mile south of the village crossroad. In early June of 2014, interior scenes of Claire and Gellis' Cranesmuir witch trial were filmed within this historic structure.

"We shot [these scenes] in order so it would feel like a real trial. Eight days in a real church in Tibbermore."

"We had almost 200 extras. They were brilliant! I love their faces. They were an important part of making it feel real."

[Tweets posted by *Outlander* producer Matthew B. Roberts on April 18th, 2015. (The premier date of *The Devil's Mark* episode shot in Tibbermore Parish Church.)]

[©2013 Scottish Redundant Churches Trust]

"[Tibbermore Parish Church] is a T-plan structure, the present form of which dates largely from 1632 and 1810. ... Despite the fact that its current appearance is largely post-medieval, there seems little reason to doubt that the church is essentially a remodeled medieval building. ... It may also be mentioned that the significant numbers of eighteenth-century memorials within the churchyard make clear that this was the long-established location of a burial place, and presumably also of a church. ... The church passed out of use for worship in 1986 [when it came into the care of the Tibbermore Charitable Trust], and since 2001 has been in the care of the Scottish Redundant Churches Trust."

arts.st-andrews.ac.uk/corpusofscottishchurches/site.php?id=157024
www.srct.org.uk/index.php/our-churches/tibbermore-church

# Outlandish Scotland Journey: Part One

[©2008 A Corpus of Scottish Medieval Parish Churches]  [©2015 @InverOutlanders] Segments.

As seen in the photo above left, the church was in an alarming state of disrepair prior to filming. According to a Special Features segment on the *Outlander* Season One, Volume Two DVD, it was "neglected and crumbing," and filmmakers "fixed up" a few things before dressing the church for the shoot. The photo above right was taken long after filming had wrapped. Though it shows the opposite end of the church from that seen in the photo above left, note the restored condition of its ceiling and walls after filming.

According to Susanne of Adventures Around Scotland—who visited in December of 2015—the *Outlander* filming fee paid to the Scottish Redundant Churches Trust was subsequently used to repair the church's roof.
http://www.adventuresaroundscotland.com/travel-blog/in-search-of-outlander-witches-and-standing-stones

Happier still, in March of 2015, a £2.2 million grant was distributed to 42 historic churches in Scotland—including Tibbermore Parish Church.
> "Grants of £10,000 to £100,000 will meet the costs of urgent repairs ... Money is also being provided for structural investigations, specialist reports and bat surveys. ... Tibbermore Church in Perthshire has been awarded £48,600."
> http://www.thecourier.co.uk/news/local/dundee/pennies-from-heaven-to-restore-scottish-churches-1.856807

Tibbermore Parish Church receives a **Might-Be-Fun** rating because:
- The church is rarely open to the public.
  Special arrangements must be made in advance to achieve entrance. Which means that you have to schedule a specific time for visiting, and cannot linger longer at any prior site on the day of your appointment.
- Why not a **Skip It** rating?
  **Reason #1:** Making the special arrangement for gaining entrance is, reportedly, rather simple. (See instructions below.)
  **Reason #2:** Diverting to Tibbermore Parish Church while enroute between **Falkland Village (Site #6)** and the **Highland Folk Museum (Site #8)** adds only

## Tibbermore Parish Church: Site #7

10 minutes to an otherwise 1 hour and 45 minute drive. If you keep your church visit to 50 minutes, stopping at this site adds only an hour to your itinerary.

That said, below are photos demonstrating what you'll see here.

[*Outlander* Season 1 screenshot (enhanced)]

From *Outlander* Chapter 25, "Thou Shalt Not Suffer a Witch to Live":
> "There were two ecclesiastical examiners, seated on padded stools behind a table … One judge was abnormally tall and thin, the other short and stout. … I mentally christened the tall one Mutt and the other Jeff."

[©2015 Susanne at AdventuresAroundScotland.com]  [©2015 @InverOutlanders] Segments.

On screen, the balcony from which the judges oversaw trial proceedings (literally), is the eastern of Tibbermore Parish Church's two galleries. Because it is accessible, you can take pix of the central area from Mutt and Jeff's point of view—the viewpoint seen in the photo above right and the screenshot below.

# Outlandish Scotland Journey: Part One

[*Outlander* Season 1 screenshot (enhanced)]

[*Outlander* Season 1 screenshot]  [©2015 Susanne at AdventuresAroundScotland.com] Segments.

The pulpit of Tibbermore Parish Church was used as the "dock" where the accused were forced to stand throughout the trial. The sadly-disintegrating fresco behind the pulpit was protected and masked with wood paneling. Because the stained glass windows flanking it commemorate WWI, the dates inscribed at the bottom (1914-1919) were obscured for filming.

The candelabras created and hung for filming are very similar to a real-world 18th century candelabra chandelier in the Culross Palace Withdrawing Room, where Geillis' parlor scenes were shot. [**Culross Village (Site #1).**]

# Tibbermore Parish Church: Site #7

[©2015 scottishcivictrust.org.uk segment (enhanced)]

If you happen to be Outlandering in Scotland during the month of September, you may be able to visit Tibbermore Parish Church on a Doors Open Day.

"Doors Open Days is an annual event that gives you the opportunity to visit historic and interesting buildings not usually open to the public, all for free. Doors Open Days takes place throughout Scotland and is part of European Heritage Days, nationally coordinated by the Scottish Civic Trust."
http://www.doorsopendays.org.uk

Use "Tibbermore Church" to search for information about Doors Open Days on the website above. Below is a portion of the 2015 schedule, when Tibbermore Parish Church was open on September 26th (Saturday) and 27th (Sunday).

"For Outlander fans on Doors Open Day Saturday, step back in time to stand in the pulpit in Claire and Geillis' fictional footsteps—if you dare. ... storyteller Amanda Edmiston of Botanica Fabula will weave a Jacobite twist into the history of the kirk with traditional folklore, tales of herbal medicine and plant lore between 11am and 1pm. ... from 1:30pm until 3pm, Scots Bard Paraig MacNeill, a singer storyteller, will use the atmospheric setting of the kirk to take you back in time to the Jacobite era with songs, rhymes, riddles and folklore."

## Learn More About Tibbermore & the Parish Church:

- https://www.scotlandschurchestrust.org.uk/church/tibbermore-church
- https://en.wikipedia.org/wiki/Battle_of_Tippermuir
- http://old.scotwars.com/battle_of_tippermuir.htm
- http://portal.historic-scotland.gov.uk/designation/BTL39

To see additional photos, go to the **Tibbermore Parish Church** board on our **Outlandish Scotland Journey Pinterest Site**:
https://www.pinterest.com/chasOSJ/tibbermore-parish-church/

# Outlandish Scotland Journey: Part One

## OutlanderLinks

All website addresses and coordinates found in this chapter (including those in the Time & Travel section, below) are available in the **Site #7 OutlanderLinks** PDF, posted free of charge on the **Part 1 OutlanderLinks** directory of our website.
http://OutlandishScotland.com/07OutlanderLinks.pdf

Updated Tibbermore Church available after *Outlandish Scotland Journey* is published will also be posted in this directory.

# Time & Travel: Tibbermore Parish Church
## Visiting Time

- As mentioned above, if you make advanced arrangements to gain entrance, spending **50 minutes** at Tibbermore Parish Church when driving between Falkland Village and the Highland Folk Museum will add only an hour to your itinerary.
- Schedule additional time if you want to wander through the 18th century graveyard surrounding this historic church.

## Opening Hours

"Access to the church can be arranged with the local keyholder. Please contact us for details. … contact@srct.org.uk"
http://www.srct.org.uk/index.php/our-churches/tibbermore-church

## Admission Fee

None. Please make a generous donation when you visit.

## Public Transportation Directions

Outlanderites using public transportation to reach Tibbermore Parish Church will need to schedule substantially more than 1 hour to visit this site.
Use Traveline Scotland to plan your trip. Your destination is "Tibbermore, Perth & Kinross."
www.travelinescotland.com
www.travelinescotland.com/apps

Both bus stops are at the village crossroad. The church is only two tenths of a mile south from there—approximately a 4 minute walk—and can be seen from the crossroad, on the east side of the lane.

## Driving Directions

**Tibbermore Parish Church Location Coordinates:** 56.39329,-3.53725
Only a small layby on either side of the church gate is available for parking. The keyholder may prefer that you park at her nearby farm.

Use the coordinates above or the keyholder's address.

# The Highland Folk Museum: Site #8

Outlander Season One Film Sites:
Episode 1's Crofter House
Episode 5's Rent Collection Villages

[©2014 VisitScotland.com segment (enhanced)]

Even if it weren't an *Outlander* film site, the Highland Folk Museum in Newtonmore is too marvelous to miss.

"The Highland Folk Museum, recognized as Britain's first mainland open air museum, opened at Kingussie in 1944. Named Am Fasgadh (The Shelter) this became the third home for founder Dr. Isobel F. Grant's renowned core collection of Highland material culture, and as a living history museum … became the inspiration for the larger Newtonmore site.

"Opened in 1995, the Newtonmore site has gone from strength to strength, proactively reflecting many aspects of Highland rural life and culture through collecting, preserving, interpreting for and interacting with individuals, groups, communities and institutions both within and beyond the Highlands."
http://www.newtonmore.com/things-to-do/in-newtonmore/local-museums/highland-folk-museum.html

# Outlandish Scotland Journey: Part One

[©2011 Paul Hermans segment (enhanced)]

Many of the 18th century crofts found here were gently dismantled from their original location—stone-by-stone, timber-by-timber—then carefully reassembled on site. Some were constructed from scratch, using only building techniques and materials available in the 1700s. Historically accurate in every detail—both inside and out—these buildings and their immediate environs were perfect for *Outlander* filming, and even more perfect for Outlandering in Scotland.

"At the Highland Folk Museum we give our visitors a flavor of how Highland people lived and worked from the 1700s up until the 1960s! We do this by displaying over 30 historical buildings and furnishing them appropriate to their time period. …

"Our site is a mile long with our 1700s Township (featuring 6 houses) at one end … our 1930s working croft at the other. We have an on site café, gift shop and a fantastic children's playground. …

"We are also home to 'Am Fasgadh' [the newest museum building, completed in 2013] storing 10,000 artifacts plus high quality meeting rooms, a research library, conservation laboratory and suite of offices. …

"Don't miss purchasing your copy of our guidebook [in the reception building], with color photos and lots of information on all our buildings across the site, it is the perfect companion to your visit."
https://www.highlifehighland.com/highlandfolkmuseum/

[©2011 Paul Hermans segment (enhanced)]

# Highland Folk Museum: Site #8

[*Outlander* Season 1, Episode 5 screenshot (enhanced)]

Several *Outlander* Season One scenes were shot in the Highland Folk Museum's 1700s Township during late March and early April of 2014. As you can see in the photo and screenshot above, most of the film sites are easily recognized when wandering through the village.

[*Outlander* Season 1, Episode 1 screenshot segment (enhanced)

Keep your eyes open for the cottage where Claire Randall first laid eyes on Jamie MacTavish—aka, James Alexander Malcolm MacKenzie Fraser. Both the exterior (above) and interior (below) of this 18th century croft were used for filming.

# Outlandish Scotland Journey: Part One

[*Outlander* Season 1, Episode 1 screenshot (enhanced)

[©2011 Paul Hermans segment (enhanced)]

Guides dressed in period costume are stationed throughout the village and will happily direct you to iconic *Outlander* film sites, such as the wool waulking area next to the "**Tipple-and-Piss**" shed.

No. They don't actually call it that. But, they should! The two *Outlander* Season 1, episode 5 screenshots and script segments below will remind you why.

# Highland Folk Museum: Site #8

**Claire:** Ugh, that's pungent. Is that hot piss?

**Donalda Gilchrest:** Yes, Claire. Sets the dye fast.

**Donalda:** Here's a wee refreshment, Claire. Ye've earned it.

**Claire:** Thank you. Oh, my god, that's got a kick to it. …

**Donalda:** All right, back to work, ladies. And we're going to need a fresh bucket [of piss].

**Claire:** You mean now?

**Donalda:** What do you think the tipple's for?

# Outlandish Scotland Journey: Part One

[©2015 Highland Folk Museum segments (enhanced)]

If you can, visit the Highland Folk Museum on an Outlander Day!
"In September 2015 the Highland Folk Museum held its first 'Outlander Day' in conjunction with the Inverness Outlanders. Lots of traditional skills were on display, including basket making, pole lathe, spinning & weaving, herbalism and cooking were all on show."
www.highlifehighland.com/highlandfolkmuseum/outlander-day-2016/

Beginning in 2016, Outlander Day is held in early June each year. Check the events page of their website to learn the dates.
https://www.highlifehighland.com/highlandfolkmuseum/events/

[©2015 Inverness Outlanders]

From the Inverness Outlanders:
"The ladies from Badenoch Waulking Group sang some wool waulking songs and we even had a go ourselves! Three of the ladies were actually in the waulking scene in *Outlander*.

"We were fortunate that Claire, the Outlander Herbalist was able to attend and gave talks about the different herbs in the 18th Century and what they would have been used for."
invernessoutlanders.wordpress.com/2015/10/19/outlander-day-in-the-highlands/

**Who is Claire, the Outlander Herbalist?**
Dr. Claire MacKay is the Scottish herbalist hired by *Outlander* producer and creator Ron Moore as a consultant for all things herbal in the show. When first contacted by Moore,

# Highland Folk Museum: Site #8

she had never read the novels. After reading them, Claire had no hesitation about coming on board.

"For me, what immediately stood out about the novels was—[Diana Gabaldon] has REALLY done her research. Impressively so. As a researcher in the field of highland history, I can tell you, it's not easy to come by many references, and I was truly inspired by the authenticity of the herb use in Diana's books."
https://www.herbalheritage.co.uk/

While consulting for *Outlander* Season One, Claire met the author and subsequently was asked to contribute a chapter on medicinal herbs to Diana's *Outlandish Companion Volume Two* guidebook—which was published in October of 2015. Diana also encouraged Claire to write a book about historic herbs.

"Presently, I am writing the *Outlander Herbal* book. An illustrated, historic guide to the use of herbs in the Scottish Highlands, expanding on scenes from the novels and giving the historic basis for the storylines."

After gaining recognition as the *Outlander* Herbalist, the National Trust for Scotland asked Claire to begin holding herbal workshops in some of their gardens. Check the events page of the Outlandish NTS properties you'll be visiting—such as the gardens of Culross Palace and Falkland Palace [**Culross Village (Site #1), Falkland Village (Site #6)**]. Watch for dates when Claire will be presenting.

If Outlander Day isn't held during your holiday, visit the Highland Folk Museum's New and Events page to learn of special events that are.

[©2015 Highland Folk Museum (enhanced)]

## Other Highland Folk Museum Areas of Interest

The 1700s Township is only one of many interesting historical exhibits to enjoy here.
"The Museum now offers a variety of reconstructed buildings ranging from ... a traditional 1930s croft, a tin school originally from Knockbain [circa 1925], a corrugated church from Culloden [circa 1900], and various trades buildings such

# Outlandish Scotland Journey: Part One

as joiners, tailors and clockmakers. Buildings are added on an annual basis to ensure that the traditional highland culture and heritage is preserved."
https://en.wikipedia.org/wiki/Highland_Folk_Museum

[©2014 Highland Folk Museum (enhanced)]

In each exhibit, you'll find cheerful and knowledgeable guides, costumed according to the era of the building. A TripAdvisor review posted by someone who visited in October of 2015 says it all.

"I took the kids here, if I'm honest, mainly for the toilets on home bound journey. Free entry, so I bought [them a guidebook]. Well, we ended up spending almost 3 hours here. The kids loved it. Spread over more than a mile there is a tractor service that can take you the full route. However, despite that being the plan, we ended up walking the whole course. Well they ran. In and out of all the old buildings. The kids were really enthusiastic to find out about different things. …

"Run mainly by volunteers and contributions, visitor donations help them maintain this wonderful heritage site. I enjoyed it so much more seeing it through kids eyes. Explaining that there was no electric, no street lights, no phones never mind mobiles, no cars, trains or planes, had them look at me as if I were storytelling. This place illustrated this historic concept to them beautifully in living splendor they could experience."
http://www.tripadvisor.com/Attraction_Review-g642239-d298100-Reviews-Highland_Folk_Museum-Newtonmore_Aviemore_and_the_Cairngorms_Scottish_Highlands_Sco.html

## Learn More About The Highland Folk Museum:

- https://www.facebook.com/HighlandFolk/
- http://www.undiscoveredscotland.co.uk/newtonmore/highlandfolkmuseum/
- http://greatscotblog.com/2014/10/16/a-day-at-the-folk-museum-starring-miss-candida-n/
- http://greatscotblog.com/2015/05/27/greatscot-rents-rocks-and-reverence-2nd-outlandish-adventure-day-14/

# Highland Folk Museum: Site #8

To see additional site photos, go to the **Highland Folk Museum** board on our **Outlandish Scotland Journey Pinterest Site**:
https://www.pinterest.com/chasOSJ/highland-folk-museum/

## OutlanderLinks

All website addresses and coordinates found in this chapter (including those in the Time & Travel section, below) are available in the **Site #8 OutlanderLinks** PDF, posted free of charge on the **Part 1 OutlanderLinks** directory of our website.
http://OutlandishScotland.com/08OutlanderLinks.pdf

Updated Highland Folk Museum information available after *Outlandish Scotland Journey* is published will also be posted in this directory.

# Time & Travel: Highland Folk Museum

## Visiting Time

- **2 hours:** This is the minimum amount of time required to visit the museum's *Outlander* film sites. Unfortunately, 2 hours only allows for a dash through the museum shop and café before or after hiking to the 1700s Township.
- **3 hours:** This is our preferred minimum timeframe, allowing for a more leisurely museum shop and café visit.
- **5 hours:** If your itinerary can afford it, schedule 5 hours (or more) here to also enjoy several of the non-*Outlander* exhibits.

## Hours of Operation

- From late March to the end of August the museum buildings and grounds are open 7 days a week, 10:30am to 5:30pm.
- In September and October, it is open 7 days a week, 11am to 4:30pm.
- Closed November through late March.

## Admission Fees

Access to all the Highland Folk Museum buildings and exhibits is free for all visitors. That said, it would be Outlandishly appropriate to donate generously when you visit.

## Public Transportation Directions

Use Traveline Scotland to plan your journey.
www.travelinescotland.com
www.travelinescotland.com/apps
Your destination is:
Highland Folk Museum, Aultlarie Croft, Kingussie Road, Newtonmore, PH20 1AY

# Outlandish Scotland Journey: Part One

## Driving Directions
**Car Park Coordinates:** 57.069694, -4.103260
**Museum Address:** Highland Folk Museum, Newtonmore PH20 1AY

## Lodging Near the Highland Folk Museum
See the Places to Stay page of the Newtonmore Community Website.
http://www.newtonmore.com/places-to-stay.html
There are 3 hostels listed in Newtonmore, as well as several B&Bs and hotels.

In the village of Aviemore, only a 22 minute drive from the museum, you'll find the Old Bridge Inn. According to an Outlander Online interview of Sam Heughan and Ron Moore, the cast and crew highly recommend the Old Bridge Inn.
http://outlander-online.com/2015/03/25/new-sam-heughan-and-ron-d-moore-interview-bts-and-stills-of-outlander-from-conde-nast-traveler/

The Old Bridge Inn, Dalfaber Road, Aviemore, PH22 1PU
http://www.oldbridgeinn.co.uk/
https://www.facebook.com/theoldbridgeinn

If Newtonmore isn't a good lodging location for your itinerary, see our **Scotland Lodging Tips** PDF.
http://OutlandishScotland.com/ScotlandLodgingTips.pdf

# Ruthven Barracks: Site #9

## An English Fortress Featured in Jacobite History
## A Taste of Ardsmuir Prison

[©2013 Meredith Coombs segment (enhanced)]

Ruthven Barracks is an English fortress built in Scotland by the government of King George II following the failed Jacobite Rising of 1715. Constructed between 1719 and 1721, Ruthven is perched atop a promontory once occupied by two different medieval castles. It originally housed approximately 120 soldiers, and stabled 28 horses.

The first troops stationed at Ruthven were tasked with maintaining local law and order, enforcing the Disarming Act of 1716, and forestalling a future Jacobite uprising. By 1745, however, the government had significantly slackened its military commitment in the north of Scotland, and only a dozen men remained stationed at the Ruthven outpost.

An estimated 2000 men took refuge at Ruthven Barracks after Culloden—possibly as many as 3000. Prior to departing, the disheartened Culloden survivors plundered and burned the fortress. Because Ruthven was never reoccupied, the remains seen today are essentially as the surviving Jacobites left them—roofless high walls surrounding floorless and bare interiors.

Ardsmuir Prison features prominently in *Voyager*, Diana Gabaldon's third *Outlander* novel. After spending seven years hiding in a miserably small cave [**The Dun Bonnet Cave (Site #17)**] following the 1746 Jacobite defeat at Culloden, Jamie arranged to be captured, so that those living at—and under the care of—Lallybroch could benefit from the reward offered for his apprehension. Thus, in 1753, Jamie was sent to Ardsmuir Prison.

# Outlandish Scotland Journey: Part One

[©2014 dayofarchaeology.com segment (enhanced)]

Unfortunately, Ardsmuir Prison doesn't exist in the real-world.
"Ardsmuir Prison is a fictional fortress located in the north of Scotland, near Coigach. ... Located three miles from the steep granite cliffs of the coast and surrounded by empty moorland, the fortress at Ardsmuir was used as a prison for fifteen years, from 1741 to 1756. ... In summer of 1756, the fortress ceased functioning as a prison when its inmates were transported to the American Colonies, with a few exceptions. ... Thereafter, the fortress housed His Majesty's [George II's] Twelfth Dragoons."
http://outlander.wikia.com/wiki/Ardsmuir_Prison

[*Outlander* Season 3 screenshot segment (enhanced)]

Ardsmuir Prison filming for *Outlander* Season 3, episode 3, "All Debts Paid," took place at **Craigmillar Castle (Site #48)** in September of 2016.

Ruthven Barracks receives a **Might-Be-Fun** rating because:
- It isn't mentioned in Diana's novels, and isn't seen in the *Outlander* Starz TV series.
- Why not a **Skip It** rating?

# Ruthven Barracks: Site #9

**Reason #1:** Ruthven Barracks is only a hop, skip, and a jump (3 miles) north of the **Highland Folk Museum (Site #8)**. Diverting to Ruthven Barracks while enroute between the Highland Folk Museum and **Inverness (Site #10)** adds only 7 minutes to an otherwise 58 minute drive. If you limit your Ruthven Barracks visit, stopping at this site adds only an hour to your itinerary.

**Reason #2:** Although never used as a Jacobite prison, Ruthven Barracks has a significant Jacobite history, and its ruins provide visitors a strong taste of what Ardsmuir Prison would have been like, had it existed in the real-world.

## Learn More About Ruthven Barracks:

- https://www.historicenvironment.scot/visit-a-place/places/ruthven-barracks/
- https://cullodenbattlefield.wordpress.com/2016/02/05/ruthven-barracks/
- https://en.wikipedia.org/wiki/Ruthven_Barracks
- http://www.undiscoveredscotland.co.uk/kingussie/ruthvenbarracks/

To see additional site photos, go to the **Ruthven Barracks** board on our **Outlandish Scotland Journey Pinterest Site**:
https://www.pinterest.com/chasOSJ/ruthven-barracks/

## OutlanderLinks

All website addresses and coordinates found in this chapter are available in the **Site #9 OutlanderLinks** PDF, freely posted on the **Part 1 OutlanderLinks** directory of our website.
http://OutlandishScotland.com/09OutlanderLinks.pdf

Updated Ruthven Barracks information available after *Outlandish Scotland Journey* is published will also be posted in this directory.

# Time & Travel: Ruthven Barracks

## Visiting Time

- **An hour** is sufficient time to fast-march up the steep incline leading from the car park to the Ruthven Barracks ruins, explore and snap a few pix, then dash back downhill to your car.
- **90 minutes** is a more reasonable amount of time to spend here—allowing for a more leisurely stroll up to the ruins, and plenty of time to snap pix.

## Hours of Operation & Admission Fees

This is an unmanaged public place without fees, guides, or facilities of any kind. Ruthven Barracks is not illuminated, so visit during the day.

## Public Transportation Directions

Use Traveline Scotland to plan your journey.
www.travelinescotland.com   www.travelinescotland.com/apps
Your destination is the Kingussie Rail Station, about a one mile hike away.

## Driving Directions

**Ruthven Barracks Location Coordinates:** 57.07222, -4.039444
There is a car park located at the base of the footpath up to the Ruthven Barracks ruins.

# Appendices

# Outlandish Scotland Extras

To provide Outlanderites with all the information important to planning an Outlandish Scotland Journey—yet keep the size of our paperback from being too large to carry conveniently while touring—we created several PDF files and posted them free of charge on the **Outlandish Scotland Extras** directory of our website.
http://outlandishscotland.com/outlandish-scotland-extras/

**Below is a list of the PDFs available.**
Just like our OutlanderLinks PDFs, Outlandish Scotland Extras will be updated whenever new information becomes available, so check back from time to time. If an updated PDF has been posted, you'll see a note in its directory entry.

> **BTW: You can help with updating!** If you have questions not answered in our Outlandish Scotland Extras, discover new info we should share with others, or find a broken link in one of our PDFs, please Email us so that we can update these files. novelholiday@gmail.com

## Outlander Insider Info

**You Can't Get There From Here**
Alas, some of the most beloved *Outlander* sites are *fictional*—places you cannot visit.

**Not Going To Go There**
Places *not* included in our Outlandish Scotland Journey travel guidebook, and why we left them out.

**Outlander Tours**
Information about the most popular and well-established *Outlander*-themed tours.

**Outlandish Site Overview Tables**
To assist you with designing your itinerary, these tables include the following information for *each* Outlandish site—in one place:
- Site Name & Number
- Site Rating
- Whether it is a Novel or Historical Location, or a Film Site
- Whether it is a National Trust for Scotland or Historic Scotland property, Privately managed, or a Free site
- Suggested Visiting Time

## Scotland Travel Tips

**UK Terminology Guide**
Many English words mean something different in the US than they do in the UK, and vice-versa. This guide includes the ones you'll most likely encounter while Outlandering in Scotland.

**International Travel Tips**
Tips important to US and other foreign national Outlanderites when traveling to Scotland.

# Outlandish Scotland Journey

**UK Car Rental and Driving Tips**
Important considerations for selecting your rental car and preparing to drive in the UK.

**Rental Car Checklist**
Save it to your smart phone, or print and pack it in your carryon, so that it's handy when you pick up your car.

**Defeating the Left-Side Driving Dilemma**
Travelers who live in right-side driving countries (the majority of the world) *will* experience episodes of anxiety and confusion when having to drive on the left side of the road in the UK. It's unavoidable. This PDF contains tips that have helped us.

**Public Transportation Links**
Major UK transportation links and travel pass information for those who prefer not to drive. Even Outlanderites who rent a car will find it more convenient to use public transportation within major cities such as Edinburgh and Glasgow.

**Free Entry Passes for Visiting Scotland**
Learn about the Historic Scotland Explorer Pass, the National Trust for Scotland Discover Ticket, and the Scottish Heritage Pass.

**Scotland Lodging Tips**
This PDF contains important tips for finding lodgings in Scotland.
Please Note: Great Site chapters sometimes include a few local lodging references.

**Telephones and the UK**
How to dial from outside or inside the UK, and international phone options available.

**UK Internet Access**
Options for connecting with the World Wide Web while in the UK, and services that should be avoided.

**UK Photography Issues**
Railway station photography rules, the value of packing an extra, cheap or disposable camera, and more.

**Rick Steves' Lost Travel Photography Tips**
Terrific travel tips related to photography equipment, as well as techniques for snapping the most interesting pix, no longer available online.

**Packing Pointers**
General packing tips, including: smart methods of baggage identification, important travel documents to copy and stash, and vital personal supplies you'll not want to forget.

**Supplies to Purchase *in* the UK**
Stuff you don't need to lug along while traveling to Great Britain, and where to cheaply purchase these items after you arrive.

# Disclaimers

Novels as popular as Diana Gabaldon's *Outlander* series inevitably generate an amazing number of unauthorized guides, philosophical essay collections, Internet-posted "fan fiction" stories, and the like. To avoid the threat of copyright or trademark infringement litigation, unauthorized *Outlander*-related publications provide at least one **Disclaimer**.
   **Below are the several important *Outlandish Scotland Journey* Disclaimers.**

## *Outlandish Scotland Journey* is an Entirely Unauthorized *Outlander*-Related Travel Guidebook

*Outlandish Scotland Journey* (hereinafter referred to as OSJ) is not authorized, approved, endorsed, licensed—nor in any other way sanctioned—by:
- Diana Gabaldon, author of the Outlander series of novels.
- Any of Ms. Gabaldon's publishers (including, but not limited to, Dell, Bantam Dell, Random House, and Delacorte Press).
- Any of the STARZ network *Outlander* television series production companies (including, but not limited to, Tall Ship Productions & Sony Pictures Television Inc).
- Any of the *Outlander* television series distributors (including, but not limited to, Starz Inc., Amazon Prime Instant Video, HBO, and Hulu).

## The Purpose of the *Outlandish Scotland Journey* Travel Guidebook

OSJ was written solely for the purpose of guiding Outlanderites (fans of Diana Gabaldon's novels and/or the STARZ network *Outlander* television series) to a variety of real-world places in Scotland:
- Locations mentioned in Diana's first three novels
   (*Outlander*, *Dragonfly in Amber*, and *Voyager*).
- Sites that inspired—or resemble—Diana's fictional location descriptions.
- Places where significant events occurred during the 1745 Jacobite rebellion.
- Scottish film sites seen on screen in the STARZ network *Outlander* TV series.

## *Outlander*-Associated Names, Places, Titles or Terminology

OSJ does not claim—nor does it intend to imply—ownership of, or proprietary rights to, any of the character or place names, titles or terminology, used or created by Diana Gabaldon within her *Outlander* series of novels, or the television series made thereof.

## Publication of *Outlander* Screenshots

**Screenshots** (aka screen-caps) are split-second, still photographs captured when playing a TV series' DVD on a computer.
   All OSJ site chapters include one or more screenshots or screenshot segments. The sole purpose of including them is to enhance the experience of Outlanderites while visiting *Outlander*-related sites. By observing screenshots while onsite, Outlanderites are reminded of the location as it was seen on screen.
   To be an effective reminder of the TV series' locales, however, the screenshots—or screenshot segments—were altered in a variety of ways so that the film site's *background* could more easily be recognized when visiting a real-world location. Thus, each screenshot's caption includes the word, "enhanced."

# Outlandish Scotland Journey

**Screenshot Copyright Captions**
The caption of every STARZ network *Outlander* TV series' screenshot or screenshot segment that appears within OSJ should officially include the following copyright caveat: "©**Sony Pictures Television Inc.**"

Because we prefer to identify the *Outlander* TV series' **season** from which each screenshot was captured—sometimes also identifying the episode number—inclusion of a Sony copyright would cause many screenshot captions to be two lines long (or longer).

**Instead, we've put the Sony copyright info HERE, to save room within the book.**

## Use of Google or Bing Maps Images to Create OSJ Site Maps

In order to assist visiting Outlanderites to find multiple locations within a single OSJ site chapter—such as the village of Culross or the city of Edinburgh—we used segments of Google or Bing map images, enhanced and augmented them, to create a few OSJ Site Maps.

While doing so, we strictly adhered to the *Google Maps and Google Earth Content Rules & Guidelines*, and ensured that the appropriate attribution credit appeared in the thumbnail-sized OSJ Site Map images published within the travel guidebook. Said credit also is clearly attributed on each of the full-sized OSJ Site Map images used to create the Outlandish Extras PDFs that we posted **free of charge** on our website.

OSJ does not claim, nor does it intend to imply, ownership of, or proprietary rights to, any of the Google Maps image segments—or **Google Street View** image segments—used within the travel guidebook or within the Outlandish Extras PDFs posted online.

Similarly, OSJ does not claim, nor does it intend to imply, ownership of, or proprietary rights to, any of the Bing map image segments used within the travel guidebook or within the Outlandish Extras PDFs posted online.

## Author vs Authors of *Outlandish Scotland Journey*

The A Novel Holiday (ANH) travel guidebook publishing company concept was solely conceived by Ms. Charly D. Miller, as was the concept of the ANH *Outlandish Scotland Journey* travel guidebook and its various eBook Parts.

While researching and writing the OSJ travel guidebook—as well as during OSJ website design—Ms. Miller was so generously assisted by other individuals, that she feels unworthy of claiming sole credit for "authoring" the text of OSJ, or the OSJ website.

Thus, **plural terms**—such as, "authors" ... "we" ... "our"—are used throughout the OSJ travel guidebook, and the OSJ website, when referring to writers or creators of same.

**For all legal purposes, however,** the A Novel Holiday *Outlandish Scotland Journey* travel guidebook—as well as each of its eBook Parts—was solely written by CD Miller. She, alone, is responsible for all content published within any OSJ travel guidebook, as well as all content posted on the ANH and OSJ websites.

**Ms. Charly D Miller hereby avows and affirms that** any and all other individuals who participated in or contributed to the researching, writing, or publication of *Outlandish Scotland Journey* travel guidebooks—as well as the OSJ website—are **indemnified and held harmless** from and against: any and all demands, claims, and damages to persons or property, losses and liabilities, including attorney's fees arising out of or caused by any form of litigation brought against the A Novel Holiday travel guidebook company, or the *Outlandish Scotland Journey* travel guidebooks, or their associated website(s).

# Acknowledgments

## Outlandish Scotland Journey Cover

Cover photo ©2012 **Ian Parker**; Evanescent Light Photography.
http://parkerlab.bio.uci.edu/evlight.htm
Cover designed by **DC Carson**.

## Outlandish Scotland Journey Logo & Website Design

Originally designed by CD Miller, our logo was significantly polished and refined by **Desirai Labrada**—the Creative Director of **Lucid Dream Designs**, our Website Design Company.
http://luciddreamdesigns.com/

Thank you to **Jeffrey Pia**, Lucid Dream Designs' Developer and the person primarily responsible for our website's vital functions.
https://www.facebook.com/LucidDreamDesigns/

## As Always, My Biggest Thank You Goes to Ms. Dina C. Carson

**I remain more grateful to DC Carson than mere words can possibly convey.**

Dina has helped with *all* my A Novel Holiday (ANH) travel guidebook projects from the very beginning—back in 2007. Without Dina's incredibly astute writing guidance and editing talents, ANH travel guidebooks would be *awful*.

My fondest wish is to someday be able to reciprocate. Unfortunately, because Dina is far more talented than I am at *everything*, it is unlikely that I'll ever be able to help her as significantly as she's helped me. Hopefully, I'll someday be able to *financially* reward her.

**Thank you, thank you, thank you, Dahlink Dina!**

## To My Personal Friends:

Each of the following people have generously contributed—in their own way—to ensuring that I can continue pursuing my ANH travel guidebook projects:

**Janet and Mike, Leeenda and Mike, Tara, Chet, Jamie, Susan and Bob.**

You guys have no idea how much I appreciate your support, and how greatly I value your friendship.

## Lastly, to Drew & Annabeth, Auntie Dot & Uncle Itchy:

*Bless You* for always believing in me!

# Photography Credits

Each photograph caption within the *Outlandish Scotland Journey* travel guidebook chapters contains the photographer's name and the year in which the photograph was taken—unless this information is unknown.

Some photos were obtained from Internet resources such as Wikipedia, Wikimedia, or Geograph, where they were posted by photographers who generously offered the photograph's commercial re-use free from copyright restrictions.

Many photos were obtained from individuals who generously granted us permission to use their images.

A few photos were obtained from Internet sources that didn't include contact information—or sources that didn't reply to our contact attempts. If we've used *your photo* without gaining permission to do so, please Email us so we can obtain permission to continue using it and properly credit you. novelholiday@gmail.com

### *Outlander* Screenshots Source
At the start of this project (2016), we used several online sources for screenshots. Since 2018, however, we have almost exclusively relied on https://outlander-online.com. Run by "a small group of fans who want the world to appreciate Outlander as much as we do," Outlander Online is an excellent resource for good-quality images. We are extremely grateful to the volunteers at Outlander Online!

### Photographers Who Generously Posted Copyright-free Images:
Alpin Stewart, Andrew Hackney, Andrew Shiva, Andy Hawkins, Anne Burgess, August Schwerdfeger, Auz, Avarim, Bill Harrison, Billy McCrorie, Brand of Amber, Brian McNeil, Buster Brown BB, Christian Bickel, Colin Hepburn, Colin Park, Conor Power, Darrin Antrobus, Dave Conner, David Kemp, David P, Finlay McWalter, Fraser Sutherland, Giannandrea, Glen Bowman, Graeme Yuill, Gregory J. Kingsley, Guillaume Piolle, Guillaume R-B, Hollandmjuk, Humphrey Bolton, J. Drevet, James F Carter, Jim Barton, John Allan, John Lindie, Jonathan Oldenbuck, Jrockley, Julesn84, Kilnburn, Kim Traynor, Lich, M J Richardson, Magnus Hagdorn, Marshall Wayne, Mehmet Karatay, Michael Garlick, Michael Hanselmann, Mike Pennington, Mn28, MSeses, Nilfanion, Osama Shukir Muhammed Amin, Paul Hermans, Peigimccann, Postdlf, Reinhard Dietrich, Renata at English Wikipedia, Rept0n1x, Rob Bendall/Highfields, Rosser1954 (2017), Saffron Blaze via www.mackenzie.co, Scotia, Shadowgate, Simonm72, SSC Elaine, StaraBlazkova, Stefan Schäfer, Stephen C Dickson, Steve Houldsworth, Supergolden, Thomas Nugent, Wknight94, Wojsyl, WyrdLight.com, XtoF, Zenit

### Photographers Who Generously Granted Us Photo-Reproduction Permission:
- Alastair Cunningham www.clansandcastles.scot
- Ali and Morag Cameron www.lochnesscottage.com
- Alistair Matheson Deepscan Cruises www.lochness.com/cruises.aspx
- Amber Linfield, www.amberlinfieldphotography.co.uk
- Andreé Poppleton www.outlandercast.com
- Andy Sweet www.stravaiging.com
- Anne-Marie Weston https://myoutlanderadventure.com
- Ashley Firth www.lellalee.com/firth-family-road-trip-carlisle-castle/

# Photography Credits

- Barbara Jean Lewis
- Bengisu Halezeroglu https://thetravelingwallflower.com/2017/03/15/scotland/
- Bill Paterson www.allaboutthescones.com/
- Bruce and Carol Conway, https://conwaytravelogue.wordpress.com/
- Callanish Camping www.callanishcamping.co.uk/
- Camilla Iversen
- Clachaig Inn www.clachaig.com/
- Connie Verzak http://tvkillstime.com/tag/outlander-master-list/
- Conny Rhode
- Daren Frankish http://european-media.eu/
- David Thompson www.thompsonontap.co.uk/
- Dawn-Marie https://loveexploringscotland.com
- Delight and Inspire www.DelightAndInspire.com
- Elspeth Thomson Slater
- Falkirk Community Trust www.falkirkcommunitytrust.org/
- Gavin Nicholson http://bikelove-scotland.blogspot.com/
- Glencoe Folk Museum; Catriona Davidson, Curator www.glencoemuseum.com/
- Gordon & Morag Menzies www.lochnesscruises.com
- Heather Holder Hill www.outlanderevangelist.wordpress.com
- Ian Parker of Evanescent Light Photography http://parkerlab.bio.uci.edu/evlight.htm, http://parkerlab.bio.uci.edu/nonscientific_adventures/Evanescent%20Light%20Homepage3.htm
- Inverness Tours www.invernesstours.com
- Jacqui Brand, http://howecrafti.co.uk/
- James Lancaster http://castlesfortsbattles.co.uk/
- Jessica Tivy, https://galleryofgardens.wordpress.com/
- Jilly, www.jillyjillyblog.co.uk/
- Jo Woolf www.thehazeltree.co.uk/
- John and Francie Nelson
- John Marsh
- Jonathan Appleton https://thedoctorwhocompanion.com/2017/12/27/blue-box-city-the-tardis-tour-of-glasgow/
- Joni Webb, http://cotedetexas.blogspot.com/
- Jordyn Acconcia http://theurbanoutlander.com/
- Julia Michrowska
- Kevin Addies https://walkingtalkingblog.wordpress.com/
- Kimberly Kahl, https://magicalmemorieswiththemouse.wordpress.com/
- Kirstie Carrick https://hauntsofmyancestors.wordpress.com
- Lisa Hsia https://satsumabug.com/
- Lisa Van Kuiken https://vkfamily.wordpress.com/
- Lorna Corall Dey https://lenathehyena.wordpress.com/2012/05/28/loanhead-of-daviot-recumbent-stone-circle/
- Lorna McInnes https://lornastearoomdelights.wordpress.com/
- Maggie Garvin www.MagsOnTheMove.com
- Mandy Tidwell https://greatscotblog.com/
- Meredith Coombs, https://whereintheworldismez.wordpress.com/

# Outlandish Scotland Journey

- Nicola, www.funkyellastravel.com
- Northeast Family Fun www.northeastfamilyfun.co.uk
- Patti Craig-Hart www.magoguide.net
- Sally Kemp
- Sami Jeskanen of Wee Walking Tours www.weewalkingtours.com
- Stewart Macfarlane pencefn.wordpress.com/2015/01/10/sights-of-central-glasgow-3-january-2015/
- Stuart Morris, www.balgoniecastle.co.uk
- Stuart O'Hara oweite.blogspot.com/2018/06/loanhead-stone-circle-daviot.html https://oweite.blogspot.com/2018/07/easter-aquorthies-stone-circle-and-loan.html
- Sue Yates https://sueyuk.files.wordpress.com
- Susan Beech https://fifewalking.wordpress.com
- Susan Smeder http://ssmeder.com
- Susanne Arbuckle, www.adventuresaroundscotland.com
- Tara Miller
- The Royal Incorporation of Architects in Scotland
- Tony Frost https://tonyscoastalwalk.co.uk/2016/01/06/day-114-culzean-castle-ayr/
- Upnorthgeorge1
- Victoria Ade-Genschow, The British Berliner, www.thebritishberliner.com
- Weir Photography Ltd www.weirphotography.co.uk
- Wolfgang Mletzko
- Y Nakanishi

**Photographers Who Could Not be Contacted (or Did Not Reply to Contact Attempts):**
Adam walkingandcrawling.blogspot.com; ahsandotcom; Anaïs Berno; Annamarie scottishmunchkin.wordpress.com; Arjayempee ; ashmcd2012; Bernard Blanc; Bert Bindels; Borders Journeys bordersjourneys.co.uk; Brian Milne dayofarchaeology.com; CA Hauglie; Cats Whiskers Tours catswhiskerstours.com; Christopher Clark; Colin Wody; Destination Stirling destinationstirling.com; Donald J MacDonald; Elenna Loughlin; farm8.staticFlickr; Feretrius; G Stewart; Gary itraveluk.co.uk; Gary P; Gregor; GSB Photography; Heatherlea B&B Glencoe; Heritage Landscape Creativity heritagelandscapecreativity.wordpress.com; Historic Houses Association hha.org.uk/; 2013uktour.wordpress.com; Ian Dawson; Isles of Glencoe Hotel; Jack Deightonsf; Jamie Burgoyne; Jimmy Graham cuboetexcuboj.blogspot.com; JM Briscoe; John Pickin; Julie King; Kakegawa of Japan; Karen Henry; Kassy Daggett; Kate Furr-Danner; Kathleen D; Kevin Hudson; Lenyas Round the Corner lenyasroundthecorner.wordpress.com; Lesley Wilson; Lesley_1990; Lyall Duffus; Magdalena Schiefermuller; Marc Melville; Marc Tilburg; Marie Poppins; McVagabonds.com; Mike Peel; Misha Maguire; Myla Laurel; Nell Macbeth; NoenkelMi; Norri; Outlander Locations outlanderlocations.com; pascott199; Patrick Fuller; Peter Holton 500px.competerholton/marketplace; Philippa Holland & Dave Palmley; Randy Plunkett; Rob C, Glasgow; Robbie Nellies; Robert A. Dalgleish; Roger Griffith; Ronnie Cameron; Sara M.; Save Gillies Hill Organization savegillieshill.org.uk; Signal Rock Cottage; Slate House Farm; Snodge; Soonwald-Liebe; sorakara-banana; St Michaels Parish stmichaelsparish.org.uk; Stephanie Bernadette; Stirling Heritage Walks; superextraawesome; Tadeusz Czesław Sinica; Tara Foster; Thomas Alexander; Tobie Stafford; Unda J; VeePresc; Wake Up and Smell the Joy http://wakeupandsmellthejoy.com; WildyDisagreeing; www.ambaile.org.uk/en; www.ArchitectsJournal.co.uk; Zoltan Tor

# Index

## A
Abbey of Ste. Anne de Beaupré  37
Ardsmuir Prison  101

## B
Badenoch Waulking Group  96
Bennet House  17
Bessie Bar's Hall  22
Beveridge, Robert (Bob)  62
Bishop Leighton's Study  5
Black Kirk  18
Bruce Fountain  64
Bruce Inn  83

## C
Campbell's Café  61
Castle Leoch's Garden  14
City of Inverness Film Site  60
Cottage Craft Centre  70
Covenanter Hotel  63
Cranesmuir  2
Cranesmuir's Black Kirk  18
Cranesmuir Witchcraft Trial  84
Crofter House in First Episode  91

## D
Dougal's Jacobite Weapons Cache  32

## E
Ear-Nailing Scenes  4
Eldridge Manor  54

## F
Farrells General Store  61
Fayre Earth Gift Shop  61
French Port of Le Havre  47

## H
H. Allingham Music  62

## I
Inverness Apothecary Film Site  67
Inverness Outlanders  96

## L
Lady Walk Wynd  67
Le Havre Port, France  47

## M
MacKay, Claire, Outlander Herbalist  96
MacRannoch's Eldridge Manor  54
McGilvrey's Boarding House  68
Mercat Cross Square  4
Mrs. Baird's Bed & Breakfast  62
Mrs. Fitz's Family Home  7

## O
Old Bridge Inn  100
Outlander Day  96
Outlander Herbalist  96
Outlanderite Oath  viii
OutlanderLinks  viii
Outlandish Scotland Extras  ix

## P
Pan Ha' Stone Houses  50
Pillory Scenes  4
Port of Le Havre, France  47

## R
Ram's Hedd Taverne  17
Red Lion Inn  23
Rent Collection Villages  91

# Outlandish Scotland Journey

## S

Scots Dumpy Hens  14
St. Fillan's Church  44
St. Serf's Church  50

## T

Tipple-and-Piss Shed  94

## W

West Kirk  18
Witch-Burning Pyre  4
Witchcraft Trial Film Site  84
Wool Waulking Scenes  94

 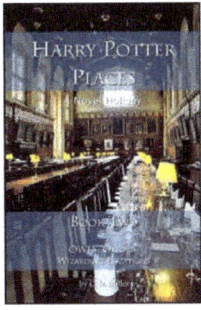 

  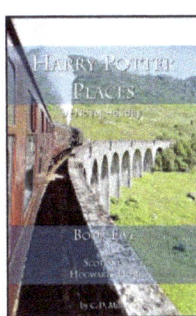

## Harry Potter Places
http://harrypotterplaces.com/

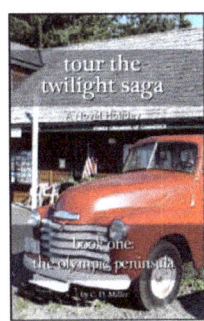  

## Tour the Twilight Saga
http://tourthetwilightsaga.com/

www.ingramcontent.com/pod-product-compliance
Lightning Source LLC
Chambersburg PA
CBHW061413090426
42742CB00023B/3460